N

SAINT BERNARD
OF
CLAIRVAUX

The Church of the Canons of Saint Vorles,
Châtillon sur Seine

SAINT BERNARD
OF CLAIRVAUX

An Essay in Biography

by
BRUNO S. JAMES

LONDON
HODDER & STOUGHTON

FIRST PRINTED 1957

Made and Printed in Great Britain for
Hodder and Stoughton Limited by
Ebenezer Baylis and Son Limited, The
Trinity Press, Worcester, and London

Nihil obstat Daniel Duivesteijn, S.T.D., *Censor deputatus*
Imprimatur E. Morrogh Bernard, *Vic. Gen.*
Westmonasterii, die 25a Februarii, 1957

INTRODUCTION

At first sight the biographer of St. Bernard is in an enviable position, for he has no lack of materials; but there lies the difficulty, for no man has been more lost sight of in his legend and achievements than Bernard of Clairvaux.

It was necessary for me to decide at the outset whether I would write a biography of Bernard or a history of his times, and I had no hesitation in choosing the former, partly because a history of Bernard and his times has already been written in French by the great Vacandard and in English by the Rev. Watkin Williams, and I doubted my ability to improve on the work of these scholars. I have contented myself with simply drawing in enough of Bernard's historical background to set his life in its proper context. It has been my constant endeavour to keep the figure of Bernard before my eyes and clear away all the matted undergrowth of irrelevant detail and legend that clings about his name like ivy round a tree. I have tried to give an impression of what sort of man he was and have only concerned myself with the momentous events of his time in so far as they have contributed to my purpose. It has not been my concern to relate every event of his life, but only such as serve to illustrate his character, and I have tried most scrupulously to adhere to ascertained facts and restrain all flights of imagination. If sometimes, led away by enthusiasm, I have let my imagination play around his figure, I have tried to make it clear that this is precisely what I am doing. It follows that of its very nature this work is an interpretation, but it is one based upon thirty years of loving study; nevertheless I do not flatter myself that it is the only possible interpretation or that better scholars than myself could not improve upon it.

The first and most obvious source of information about Bernard is the biography, commonly known as the *First Life*, written by his disciples and friends. It is a composite work; of its five books the first written by William of St. Thierry, the second by Arnald of Bonneval and the last by Geoffrey of Auxerre. There is a sixth book written some time afterwards called the *Liber Miraculorum*, but I have not enlarged on the miracles of Bernard, not because I think they are all of them questionable but simply for the reason that they seem to add little or nothing to our knowledge of his personality. Besides the *First Life* there are two others written by Bernard's friend Alan, Bishop of Auxerre, and by John the Hermit.

These early biographies are quite essential for anyone who would make a serious study of Bernard's life, but their value is limited precisely because the authors lived too close to their subject: great men like great mountains need to be seen from a distance. Moreover, these lives were written with a view to Bernard's canonization, their aim is to edify rather than to inform, and their concern is almost solely with his virtues and miracles, so that the picture they give is apt to be flat and characterless without high-lights because lacking in shadows. No Saint is free from human frailty and it is just these human frailties that bring him within the range of human understanding and sympathy; Bernard was not a disembodied spirit, he was all the more a holy man for being so very much a whole man. Besides these contemporary lives there are Bernard's own writings which may be divided into treatises, sermons, and letters. His treatises are full of interest and their doctrine is as vital today as it was in his own time, but they are chiefly of interest to those more concerned with his teaching than his personality. If this rather modest book should lead anyone on to reading them so as to discover what he taught, then it will have fulfilled its object. His sermons are in a different category; they are very wonderful in their way but to appreciate them a trained palate is necessary. It is highly doubtful whether they were ever preached as we have them, more probably they were severely edited by Bernard himself before publication. Lastly we have his letters, not by any means all of them but probably as many of them as his contemporaries wished us to have and a few more that, thanks to such scholars as Hüffer and, in our day, Dom Jean Leclercq and Dr. Talbot, have escaped this censorship. These letters have been my main source, for here, in spite of everything, we do have a picture of the man, a vivid and animated self-portrait, reflecting without pose or self-consciousness his every passing mood and feeling. Here, indeed, we have no plaster Saint, but a man who, like ourselves, but, alas, so differently from most of us, had to contend with ill health, moods of depression, fits of irritation with fools, and natural indignation with the petty persecutions of small-minded ecclesiastical bureaucrats.

Besides these and other primary sources, I am deeply indebted to many modern works, especially to the lives by Vacandard and Watkin Williams, and to the *Bernard de Clairvaux* compiled by the members of the Trappist Historical Commission. Not all these works have been listed in the bibliography for there seemed no point in mentioning books that are hardly obtainable by the average reader or that have served merely to confirm impressions and opinions derived from other sources. I am also deeply indebted to several scholars for the help they have given me, especially to Dom Christopher Butler, the Abbot of Downside, who has read through large parts of the manuscript and made several useful suggestions, and to the well-known writer Mr. Lancelot Sheppard who has most patiently read every word of this work and helped me with his experience to handle the rather formidable mass of materials. I must also express my thanks to Mr. Mark Hamilton of Messrs. Heath & Co. for his help and encouragement. Finally I wish to thank Messrs. Burns and Oates for allowing me to use my own translation and edition of Bernard's letters. Nevertheless I take full responsibility for the opinions expressed in this book; they are completely my own and I am not indebted for them to anyone. This is not a big book but, if I may adapt a well-known saying of Seneca, it has been a case of "parvum opus, magnus labor". I have been at immense pains to keep it within very reasonable bounds not merely for the sake of economy but chiefly so that the subject should not be obscured by a mass of more or less irrelevant detail. This has meant constant pruning and re-writing. It has not had an easy birth for it is the work of an inexperienced writer, and it has been written in several different parts of the world, some of it in England, some of it in the south of Italy not far from where Bernard confronted Count Roger, and very much of it while wandering in Burgundy.

Note. The reference to the letters follows the enumeration in my own translation with that of Migne in brackets.

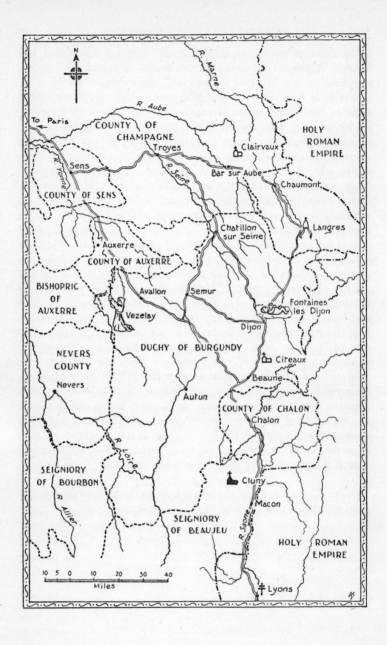

CHAPTER I

In a small bare room in the year 1153 a monk lay dying and all Christendom mourned. He was Bernard of Clairvaux. During the last forty years of his life he had dominated the whole Church. His words had resounded throughout Europe; and in France, Germany, and Italy men had left their homes to follow him and embrace the hard life of a Cistercian monk. He had sent his disciples to found monasteries in the furthest corners of Western civilization. He had counselled and sometimes fearlessly rebuked popes and kings, and he had upheld the cause of the poor and succoured the widow and the orphan. He had healed a schism in the papacy, made peace between warring armies, and single-handed he had grasped the discordant elements of Europe, welded them into a united body, and hurled them against the Saracen. Yet he had never ceased to be before all else a monk and a mystic who would return to his monastery from the Court of Rome and from dealing with high matters of state, continue calmly with his sublime sermons on the Song of Songs.

Did his thoughts dwell on anything of this as he lay there dying on the boards of that mean room? We do not know. The only record we have of those solemn moments is the letter he wrote from his death-bed to a friend: "Pray our Saviour, who wills not the death of a sinner, that he may watch over my passing. Support, I beg you, with your prayers a poor wretch destitute of all virtue, so that the enemy who lies in wait for me may find no place where he can grip me with his teeth and wound me."

It is the purpose of this biography to portray the man who could thus write his will across the world and yet remain before all else a mystic and a monk. His actions belong to the history of his time and his teaching to the theology of the Church. These will be examined here only for the light they can throw on his personality.

II

St. Bernard of Clairvaux was born at Fontaines lès Dijon in

Burgundy during the year 1090[1] and he died sixty-three years later in his monastery at Clairvaux. If we wish to understand him we must try to see him against the background of his times and to form some idea of the faith and ideals that coloured his whole life. Although his example and his doctrine are valid for all time and although he was in many respects far in advance of his contemporaries, yet he remained all his life a child of the Middle Ages. The first half of the twelfth century is often spoken of as the age of St. Bernard but he could not have influenced his age so deeply had he not belonged to it so thoroughly. It was an age so different from ours that it is only with the greatest difficulty that we can understand it. The ideals and values that inspired the society of that time differ so widely from those that prevail today that it is not at all easy for a modern man to appreciate them or even to form an objective view of them. And we are very different people from the men and women of the twelfth century. It is often said that times change but human nature remains the same, but this is only true in the broadest sense. There can be little doubt that the nature of at any rate us Western Europeans has changed considerably during the last eight hundred years. We are more disciplined, less passionate and what, for want of a better word, we can only call more refined than our forefathers of the Middle Ages.

We hear very little of the battles of Lech and Mecklinberg in which during the year 955, just over a hundred years before St. Bernard, Otto the Great utterly routed the Magyars and Wends. Yet for the respite that these decisive victories gave to the peoples of Western Europe in which to develop their highly complex society, they rank in importance hardly lower than the battle of Marathon. With the defeat of the Magyars and Wends and with the decline in the raids of the Northmen expectation of life increased and the arts of peace began to flourish. Agriculture, the staple industry of those days, was still primitive in the time of Bernard but waste lands were being brought under the plough and new methods of cultivation were being discovered. Commerce had begun to flourish and to bring within the reach of those that could afford them luxuries

[1] There seems to be little doubt about this date. It is based on the statement of William of St. Thierry that Bernard entered Citeaux in the year 1113 when he was about twenty-three years old. There is however a tradition that he was born at Châtillon-sur-Seine where his family undoubtedly had a house, but other evidence establishes Fontaines lès Dijon as the place of his birth to the satisfaction of most of the leading authorities.

undreamed of since the fall of Rome. Learning and literature were reviving and soon the rise of Peter Abelard in the schools of Paris would herald the passing of the old ways of thought and the dawn of scholasticism. It was an age of intense intellectual curiosity and activity. Young men would traverse the whole continent, begging their way as they went, in order to sit at the feet of some famous master. Questions of philosophy and theology were eagerly discussed and as much interest was shown in them as in scientific development nowadays. It was possible for a subtle philosopher and theologian like Abelard to set Europe by the ears with his novel intellectual approach to old problems and it was one of Bernard's complaints about him that he had set the crowds in the market place discussing the mysteries of the faith. Slowly the Church was shaking herself free from the shackles of the State and from the burden of lay patronage. The movement began in the year 1049 when Pope Leo IX summoned a Council at Rheims and before the exposed relics of St. Remigius and a vast concourse of people struck consternation in the hearts of the assembled Bishops and Abbots by deposing all of them who had obtained their position by virtue of their money. And since then zealous popes inspired by the spirit of reform had endeavoured to curb the secular influence on the Church and eliminate from the Sees men who owed their position in it to the length of their purses or the strength of their supporters. Much still remained to be done in Bernard's day and much would remain undone, but by the twelfth century men of profound learning, high ideals, and saintly life such as William of Champeaux, Bishop of Châlons-sur-Marne, were becoming increasingly common amongst the prelates of the Church.

The feudal society of the day was based on the land and divided into four classes: the nobility, the clergy, the burgesses and the serfs. The life of even the highest nobility was crude and rough by our standards and so too often were their manners. But here the scene, like so much in the Middle Ages, is full of colourful contrasts. Some of the nobility seem to have been little better than brigands while others, like Bernard's friend Theobald Count of Blois, were men of extreme piety and the highest integrity. Robert 1st, Duke of Burgundy from 1032 until 1076, is a good example of the former. Amongst other crimes he had his brother-in-law murdered and killed his father-in-law with his own hands. Yet his successor became a monk and died in what is commonly called the odour of sanctity. But by Bernard's day the influence of the Church, as well, perhaps, as the growing luxury of the age had begun to soften their manners.

The growth of towns and the increasing power of the communes were a feature of the age. The demand for luxuries which could only be obtained by trade and for ready money to buy them which could only be obtained from the Jews brought great prosperity to the merchants and to those who lent out money at interest. The more enlightened landlords encouraged commerce if only to exploit it to greater advantage, and they were sometimes wise enough to try to influence rather than to suppress the growing power of the communes; but the burgesses were not infrequently able to extort by force the privileges they were unable to obtain by complaisance. The lot of the serfs was still hard by our standards, but they were more often only serfs in name. There are cases on record of serfs selling property at a good price to their lords and even of free men voluntarily offering themselves and their families as serfs to the great monasteries. They enjoyed a fixed tenure for themselves and their sons and they were protected by custom and also by the Church. The self-interest of their lords assured for them a roof over their heads, food on their tables, and a fire in their hearths. If they wished to leave the land and could remain under the protection of one of the towns for a year and a day they were quit of all obligation to their lord. No doubt that their life was harder and rougher than the life of our own farm labourers and factory workers, but their food was probably more wholesome and their status as human beings with spiritual as well as material needs more fully recognized. Amenities, sanitation, and comfort as we understand them were quite unknown to the serfs of the twelfth century, but in this they were no differently situated from everyone else.

It is true that life in those days remained, in spite of all that was beautiful, rough and dangerous. Disease and filth were all but universal. Wars and local turmoils were brutal and common. In the heat of battle convents and churches were sacked, treasures destroyed, nuns raped and men mutilated. But if the romantic medievalist with eyes for nothing but the colour and glory of the high Middle Ages sees only part of the picture, he is less mistaken than the modern materialist who sees nothing but the squalor and filth and cannot understand why the people of those days built glorious churches while living in poverty themselves. We shall never begin to understand the period unless we have some comprehension and some appreciation of the faith that not only inspired the poetry and superb buildings of the time but was also part of the very mental fibre of the men and women of the day and which permeated their whole outlook and values. Poverty and disease were widespread but poverty was not considered a disgrace or physical suffering as the only, or even as the greatest, evil. The supernatural was woven into the very fabric of life and lent nobility and hope to the most wretched. This is not to say that everyone spent his time in church or dancing round the maypole. As we have seen it was a time of violent passions and grievous crimes. But men knew what sin was and there was no one so powerful that his crimes could not be brought home to him in the end. Nor must we think that the moral lapses and folly of the clergy or even of the popes escaped comment. Indeed, men for the very reason that they were so sure of their faith were far more outspoken in the criticisms of the pope than would be possible nowadays without incurring grave suspicion of disloyalty. Bitter and even scurrilous satires on the lives of the clergy and on the manners of the papal court were at times widely current. The popular "Gospel according to the Mark of Silver" might have come from the pen of a rabid modern anticlerical. And yet except for a tiny minority of cranks it never occurred to anyone in those days to question the supernatural origins of the Church. It was because they believed so strongly that they could criticize the shortcomings of popes and clergy so savagely.

And so we see the age of St. Bernard spread out before us like a cloak of many colours in which the golden threads of faith, aspiring idealism, heroic sanctity, high intellectual endeavour and great artistic sensibility are contrasted with the more sombre shades of violence, passion, ignorance, and squalor, but of which the general aspect and shape is a thing of great beauty.

III

It is only the slightest of exaggerations to say that the history of France is the history of all Europe and that she is the second home of every civilized European. The past seems to cling about her countryside, and the names of her ancient towns and villages shine like gems in the stuff of history. Here Vercingetorix made his last

stand against the armies of Rome; here lies, so men say, the body
of St. Benedict, the Father of Monks; here in all the glory of the
High Middle Ages the Kings of France were anointed and crowned;
and here St. Bernard with words of fire preached the Crusade
and inflamed the hearts of men with the love of Christ so that they
deemed all the glory of the world no better than dung! The list
seems endless for the beginnings of it are lost in the mists of legend.
Perhaps there is no other country in Europe to which those well-
known lines of Virgil in which he lovingly describes the ancient
cities of Italy can be so well applied as to France.[1] And if this is true
of the country as a whole it is especially true of Burgundy. There
are many other parts of France that have a more direct and dramatic
appeal but no one with any historical sense at all can fail to be moved
as he wanders through the old townships of Burgundy, and no one
with any sense of beauty can travel through the gracious and fertile
countryside with its rich fields, famous vineyards, and old red-
roofed manor houses, and remain insensible to its charm. Something
of the past certainly lingers here amongst these quiet woods and
fields. All this is as true of Dijon, the rich capital of the province,
as it is of the small walled towns of the hills and valleys. Much of
Dijon is quite modern. Motors and buses fill the gay and crowded
streets with their din. But an atmosphere of the Middle Ages still
seems to hover and eddy around her old courtyards, dim alleys and
solemn buildings, where the noise and bustle of the busy streets is
muted and only the church bells stir the silence.

The traveller who approaches Dijon along the road from Châtillon will notice on his left before he comes within sight of the city
over the fields of cassis and fruit trees the towers of the Château of
Fontaines lès Dijon with, if he is fortunate and the day is very clear,
the great crest of Mt. Blanc heaving over the far horizon like a
broken wave. Here at Fontaines lès Dijon St. Bernard was born
and hereabouts he must have wandered as a child and along this
very road he must have passed on his way to school at Châtillon.
Nothing authentic remains of the castle of Bernard's father, but the
view with Mt. Blanc in the distance would not have changed.
The comparatively modern building which occupies the site of
Bernard's home incorporates a large chapel dedicated to him. This

---

[1] "Adde tot egregias urbes operumque laborem
Tot congesta manu praeruptis oppida saxis,
Fluminaque antiquos subterlabentia muros." Vir. Georg. II, 155-8.

building has been embellished regardless of cost or taste and it has nothing to tell us of Bernard. But the small romanesque Church on the left as one faces the Château speaks far more clearly of him, and they will even show the unwary or credulous traveller the font at which they say he was baptized.

IV

If we want to picture to ourselves Bernard's home as it really was we must put out of our minds any idea of one of those great castles with which imposing ruins have made us familiar. Bernard's home was little more than a stone keep in which the family lived with a rather primitive wall around it and, as a first line of defence, a deep ditch or moat.[1] Of course all this has crumbled away long ago, and only the hill on which it stood remains.

The father of Bernard was Tescelin, surnamed the Sor (Sorrh) on account of his reddish complexion. Brave and ingenious attempts have been made to trace his ancestry, but the results are purely hypothetical and do not tell us anything about his son.[2] It seems probable that he was one of the Knights of Châtillon, of ancient and honourable stock but not one of the highest of the land. He had the reputation of being a brave and honourable knight, full of zeal for justice. More than this nothing can be said for certain. But through his mother Bernard was certainly connected with many of the most noble families in Burgundy. She was Aleth the daughter of Bernard of Montbard who seems to have been connected with the Counts of Bar-sur-Seine, and on his mother's side with the Lords of Couches. Gaudry her brother, who was later to follow Bernard to Citeaux, had become by marriage Lord of the castle of Touillon. From the little that we know of her Aleth seems to have been a

---

[1] ". . . a feudal stronghold, the patriarchal home of a great and noble family under whose benign protection lay safely sheltered at its feet the few folk to whom its lord was at once the father and the chieftain," Watkin Williams, *Studies in St. Bernard of Clairvaux*. With all respect for the learned author this description is more enthusiastic than accurate. More precisely M. Jean Mariller in "Bernard de Clairvaux. Les premiers années. Commission d'Histoire de l'Ordre de Citeaux:" ". . . le château de Tescelin n'était qu' une motte forte, un 'minus castrum'."

[2] He was one of the "milites Castellionenses" . . . a group of knights attached to a fortified town for its defence, in this case to Châtillon. Some of the knights came from rather modest families and had obtained the "cingulum militiae" in return for faithful service to their lord; others were men of substance and sometimes cadets of noble houses.

woman of strong character. She had been destined by her parents
for the cloister, but when the Lord of Fontaines asked for her hand
in marriage she accepted him and lived in the world more like a nun
than the châtelaine of a distinguished knight. Without neglecting
her duty to her husband and children she devoted all the time she
could spare to her devotions and the poor. There could not have
been much time to spare for she had seven children, six sons and one
daughter, of whom Bernard was the third. Their names in order of
birth were Guy, Gerard, Bernard, Hombeline, Andrew, Bartholomew, and Nivard. She would have no help in the care of them
and nursed every one of them herself. There is a legend that before
the birth of Bernard Aleth dreamed that she bore in her womb a dog
that kept on barking and was told by a hermit that it meant she
would give birth to a child who would become a great preacher and
bark loudly in defence of the Church.[1] In those days children were
confided entirely to the care of the women and saw very little of
their father and there can be no doubt that Bernard's mother had a
very strong influence on his character. If we only knew more about
her we might be in a better position to understand her son, but
unfortunately we search his early biographies in vain for any clear
and living clue to the character of Aleth. Beyond the usual stereo-
typed and turgid platitudes they tell us little that is relevant.

Bernard seems to have been marked out by his parents for a
career in the Church while he was still quite a child, and while his
brothers were learning to ride and hunt and give and receive hard
blows he was sent off to school with the Canons of St. Vorles at
Châtillon. Châtillon is about fifty miles North of Dijon. Tescelin
had a house there and the family home of Aleth was hardly twenty
miles away at Montbard. The small church of St. Vorles still
stands at Châtillon[2] and there is in the crypt an ancient shrine of
Our Lady, which the guide claims to date from the sixth century,
where the young Bernard used to pray. Here he would have been
taught to read and write, to recite the psalms by heart and to chant
them. There is a legend that on Christmas Eve when he was seven
years old, just before the Mattins of the feast, he had a vision of the
birth of Christ. William of St. Thierry, one of his first biographers,
says that this vision left a lasting impression on Bernard and that he

---

[1] William of St. Thierry has embroidered this story.
[2] Alas! it is in a shocking condition (1956): the plaster-covered walls scribbled all
over with sometimes indecent inscriptions. Mass is said there once a month.

was always convinced that he had had it at the same hour as Our Lord's birth.[1]

As there is no evidence to the contrary it seems probable that Bernard remained with the Canons of St. Vorles for his higher studies. These would have comprised grammar, rhetoric, and dialectic. There is no real evidence that he ever knew Greek but he had certainly studied the usual Latin authors very thoroughly and also that rather tedious and fanciful work on etymology by St. Isidore of Seville. We are told that he was an exceptionally brilliant pupil and everything we know of him bears this out. Berengarius, a disciple of Bernard's opponent Peter Abelard, declared that he distinguished himself at St. Vorles by composing ribald verses. There is no inherent improbability in this, but the statement stirred up such a storm of protest from Bernard's disciples, who would not tolerate anything but what they considered edifying, that Berengarius was obliged to withdraw his rash statement.[2]

Some idea of Bernard's appearance and character at this time can be gathered from the stilted and conventional phrases of his early biographers. He was tall and blonde and clearly exceptionally handsome. His most striking feature seems to have been his eyes, but as we are only told that they were "dove-like" it is not easy to say what colour they were. Is it possible that he was an albino or would this be pressing the metaphor too hard? He had many friends and was known for his urbanity and charm. Undoubtedly he was a young man of outstanding personality giving early promise of that extraordinary personal fascination which in later life even his opponents could not withstand. In spite of his urbanity he was apparently so sensitive and shy at this age that he could hardly be persuaded to open his mouth in front of strangers. He was to remain extremely sensitive all his life, but not dumb even before strangers.

[1] It is probably this which is at the root of the charming but baseless legend of the "lactation of St. Bernard" current in the sixteenth century.

[2] This statement of Berengarius has the ring of spite about it. The learned M. Marillier (op. cit.) believes that the foundation of it may lie in the "dictamina" or exercises in Latin composition, which need not necessarily have had a religious theme, that were required of young scholars. There are however indications in the writings of St. Bernard that there were incidents in his youth which he regretted. Too much must not be built on the humble avowals of a Saint; on the other hand although Saints feel the guilt of their sins more poignantly than other men, they do not invent them. All the writings of Bernard indicate a passionate and highly emotional nature, at the time of his maturity perfectly under discipline but perhaps not always so. The very extremes of asceticism to which he went could indicate the fierce battle he had to bring himself to order.

Like so many sensitive people he suffered from his earliest youth from what we should now call megrims. He had frequently to retire suffering from severe headache. On one of these occasions (Aleth must have been away or she would never have permitted it) a local wise-woman was called in to charm the pain away. But young Bernard would have none of her and leapt from his bed and drove her from the room. Already in the youth one can discern the lineaments of the Abbot of Clairvaux! He appears to have been very devout at this time but if we may deduce the child from the character of the grown man there was never anything of the prig in Bernard. A youth of great good looks, charm, and intelligence, but undoubtedly full of high spirits and gaiety as any healthy youth should be. He did not escape the usual temptations of adolescence nor is there any reason at all why he should have done, but we can believe he passed through the crisis unscathed. A youth of such charm and looks could hardly expect to escape the admiration and attentions of the other sex, and we are told that on one occasion he threw himself into a pond of icy water to calm the tempest of his passions after he had allowed himself to exchange admiring glances with a girl who was passing.[1]

On the first of September, the feast of St. Ambrosian, the patron of Fontaines, in the year 1104, the mother of Bernard died. It had been her custom to summon all the clergy of the neighbourhood to her house on that day and wait on them herself. But this year she fell seriously ill on the eve of the feast and felt that her life was drawing to an end. She summoned Guy, her eldest son, warned him of her condition and told him to gather the family around but on no account to put off the coming festivities. Then after receiving the Viaticum, while her family were reciting the prayers for the dying, she rendered her soul to God. Her friend Jarentin, the Abbot of St. Benignus at Dijon, received her body and buried it with great honour in the crypt of his church where it remained until the year 1250 when it was removed to Clairvaux and reinterred before the altar of St. Saviour in the Abbey church.

Bernard took the shock of his mother's death very hardly. She had been the main influence in his life. It was she who had inspired

---

[1] Another story is told of how when Bernard was staying in a neighbour's house, his hostess tried to enter his bed at night, and Bernard saved the situation and put the woman to confusion by calling out that thieves had entered his room. As this story is part of the regular stock-in-trade of the medieval hagiographist its authenticity is open to suspicion.

him with the desire to serve God either as a monk or as a priest and it was she who had insisted on his being educated for the Church. It is not surprising that he was stunned by her death and lost for a time the sense of high purpose which she had fostered in him. Yet it was not to be long before her influence over him was to be reasserted in a striking and dramatic manner.

CHAPTER II

Not much is known of Bernard between the year 1104 when his mother died and 1111 when he definitely made up his mind to become a monk. It is to be assumed that he continued his studies at Châtillon.

No one was very surprised at his wanting to be a monk. It had always been more or less taken for granted in the family that he would want to go into the Church. He had been educated with this end in view. But everyone was very surprised indeed when he declared his intention of becoming a monk at Citeaux instead of one of the opulent houses of Black Monks in the neighbourhood. Citeaux[1] was a poor and insignificant house founded some years previously in an unwholesome swamp about fifteen miles the other side of Dijon. The place had not prospered. The founder, St. Robert, had left it after six months there. It had enjoyed a certain *réclame* just after its foundation and several young men of good family had tried the life but very few had persevered and since then a number of the monks had died—from fever and undernourishment, people said—and the house seemed on the point of closing down. The life was hard, the community poor, and the situation unhealthy. Not at all the place for a delicate and bookish young man like Bernard.

At first sight this austere choice of Bernard does appear surprising. Cluny would have seemed the obvious place for him. He had kinsmen in the community and the life was regular but not over-severe. His literary gifts would have had ample scope and, with the backing of his family, he might have made quite a career for himself there. Monks of Cluny had risen very high in the hierarchy of the Church before now and some of them had become great statesmen.

Learned men have tried to investigate his reasons for choosing Citeaux and their lengthy disquisitions and edifying conclusions would have been more plausible if Bernard himself had not given us the answer. After enlarging on the glories of Cluny he says: "Someone may say to me: 'If you think so highly of Cluny why did you

---

[1] The name may perhaps be derived from "Cistel", the local word for the rushes that grew in that swampy district.

not become a monk there?' My reply to this is that I did not become a monk of Cluny because, in the words of the Apostle, 'I am free to do what I will; yes, but not everything can be done without harm.' I chose Citeaux in preference to Cluny not because I was not aware that the life was excellent and lawful but because 'I am a thing of flesh and blood, sold unto the slavery of sin'. I was conscious that my weak character needed a strong medicine."[1] This explanation which he gives us with all the candour of a really humble man is very revealing for those whose eyes are not blinded by a preconceived notion of sanctity.

The first person to whom Bernard confided his intention of entering Citeaux was his Uncle Gaudry of Touillon. Gaudry listened sympathetically to what his nephew had to say because he too had been wanting to do something of the same sort. But it was not so simple for him because he was married. They decided to keep the matter a secret for the time being. Yet it was not long before Bernard's brothers guessed that there was something in the air. Great was their outcry when they heard the truth. We may plausibly imagine something of what they thought and said. "It was bad enough that Bernard should want to become a monk, but then what could one expect of a young man who had spent his time poring over books instead of learning how to fight and hunt? Nevertheless it was unthinkable that he should want to join that band of madcap enthusiasts at Citeaux. Why, the life there would kill him! Monks had been dying there like flies. Besides it would be a wicked waste of his gifts. If he must become a monk then let him join one of the great houses of Black Monks in the neighbourhood. Everyone knew about them and many people had kinsmen there. The life might be dull, but it would not kill him, and he would have scope for his literary work. But what possible good could come of his carting manure at Citeaux?" These may not have been their exact words but, from what we know of them, they probably said something like this. At length Bernard gave way to them so far as to agree to postpone any final decision until he had been to Germany to finish his literary studies. This was a shrewd suggestion of his family because Bernard had always cherished literary ambitions. It has been said that he gave up everything when he became a monk except the art of writing well. Certainly he did more than anyone else in his lifetime to raise the standard of literary

[1] Apology: c. 4 vii.

taste. For command of Latin prose and lucid self-expression he had no rivals in his day.

In the autumn of that year Bernard was at Châtillon making ready for his departure to Germany. Before leaving he set out to say good-bye to his brothers who, in the service of their suzerain, were occupied in besieging the Château of Grancy. We may still visit the Château there, parts of it said to be coeval with St. Bernard, and if we are so minded we can still follow the same road that Bernard took to it. It passes through some of the most lovely country in Burgundy, winding between wooded hills and green fields with every now and then small streams scampering through them. It cannot have changed so very much since Bernard's day. At the time that he made the journey the leaves would have begun to turn and there would have been the smell of burning wood in the air. During his leisurely progress he pondered on his plans for the future, not at first very feverishly, but as a man does when he is riding through pleasant country and in no great hurry. The rhythm of horses' hooves encourages thought. Quite suddenly he began to feel uneasy about it all. He wondered what his mother would think. Then all at once he thought he saw her standing by the roadside, looking at him sorrowfully. He dropped into a small chapel that stood near by. We do not know what went on in the cool shadows of that small chapel but we can guess from what transpired afterwards that Bernard must have had a sharp fight with himself. He came out into the sunlight a man transformed. There would be no more hesitation. His mind was made up. He would not go to Germany, he would give up all thought of a literary career, he would offer himself at once to Citeaux. That was what his mother would have expected of him and that was what he would do. He must steel his heart against his brothers' sorrow at losing him and against his own sorrow at parting with them. But no! He would do better than that, he would take them all with him. He would do just that and they would not be able to resist him. It takes a very young man to make a wild plan like this and it takes a Bernard to achieve it.

He arrived at Grancy boiling with enthusiasm for his mission and rejoicing in his new-found strength only to discover that his brothers Guy and Gerard were not there. They had set off that morning to find him at Châtillon and must have missed him on the road when he was in the chapel. So he went straight to his Uncle Gaudry's tent.

Gaudry, catching his enthusiasm, declared he would join him as soon as his wife had given her permission. Then they both went off to find Tescelin and acquaint him with their plan. Tescelin made no difficulties at all, but he was probably relieved that Gaudry would be there to keep his son's enthusiasm within reasonable bounds. Bartholomew was present at the time and was easily prevailed upon by Bernard to follow him. Then Bernard set out to look for Andrew. Andrew had just been dubbed a knight but had rather unfortunately been taken prisoner in his first encounter with the enemy. This did not deter Bernard. Somehow or other he gained access to him. As he began to talk about Citeaux Andrew cried out that he saw his mother standing at his brother's side, whereupon Bernard, who never missed an opportunity, told him that this proved it was their mother's wish that he should come with him to Citeaux. Andrew capitulated but on the condition that all his brothers should come too, "otherwise," he said, "you will have to cut me in half for I cannot live without them or endure to be separated from you!"

When Guy and Gerard heard of their brother's new resolution they accepted the inevitable and gave up trying to dissuade him. But this was not enough for Bernard, he told them that they must come with him. Guy replied that this was impossible, he could not leave his wife and family. Bernard answered that if he put himself in the right dispositions he would be released from his marriage either by the consent of his wife or by her death. Rather taken aback by this but feeling quite sure of his ground Guy said that if such a thing happened he would agree to enter Citeaux. Then he set off to see his wife and talk the matter over with her. His wife met him at the door in tears and begged him to allow her to enter a convent. Bernard must have got there before him. After this there was nothing more that Guy could do: he had given his word and was committed to Citeaux.

There still remained Gerard and he was to prove more difficult. He simply brushed all Bernard's arguments aside as hare-brained follies. It is difficult not to sympathize with him. But Bernard was not to be gainsaid. He had recourse to that rather disconcerting gift of prophecy he was to use in later life with such effect. "You are closing your heart to the grace of God," he told Gerard, "but it will find a way in through a wound in your side." We have no record of what Gerard replied to this. A fortnight later he was wounded in the side and taken prisoner. Scared by his condition as well as by the unexpected fulfilment of his brother's prophecy he cried out that he was a monk of Citeaux. The enemy put him under lock and key just the same. It was an age of faith but this was rather too much for them to believe. They held on to him as a hostage. He appears to have been more closely watched than Andrew for even Bernard could not get near him and had to content himself with shouting words of encouragement through the window. "We are all just off to Citeaux," he cried, "but unite your heart with ours and you will be a monk at least in intention." Gerard must have been very thoroughly converted if he found any encouragement in this.

Bernard was not for long content with persuading merely his brothers to follow him, he very soon decided that all his friends must come too. While he was travelling the countryside gathering into his net everyone he could, his brothers waited at Châtillon preparing themselves by prayer and solitude for their great venture. As we would say, they were making a "retreat". One day Bernard announced to them that he was going to bring his friend Hugh of Mâcon along. His brothers were a little dubious about this. Hugh of Mâcon was a young nobleman who had become a cleric at Vitry and he was very comfortably situated in the enjoyment of several rich benefices. It did not seem at all likely that he would want to join them. They liked the young man but could not see him as a monk at Citeaux. In any case it was more than doubtful if his brother clergy would let him go. Young noblemen were an acquisition to the clerisy. But Bernard did not let any considerations like this stand in his way and he set out to interview Hugh without delay. It did not take him long to reduce this young man to tears and acquiescence. The problem was to get Bishop and Chapter to agree. There was to be a synod in a few days and Hugh thought it would be a good plan to take this occasion for publishing his decision to enter Citeaux with Bernard. When the day came Bernard was present to keep his friend's courage up. But the clergy had got wind of his activities on behalf of Citeaux and would not allow him to get near Hugh. However, Providence seemed to take a hand in the matter. A great storm broke and (the synod was being held *sub dio*) the clergy scattered. In the confusion Bernard button-holed his friend and asked what had happened. Hugh replied that he had promised not to become a monk for a year but that this need not prevent him accompanying Bernard to Citeaux because it would be a full year before he would take his vows. This is what some of Bernard's biographers describe as a "pious fraud" but history does not record what the clergy thought of it. Once more Bernard was able to return in triumph "carrying his sheaves with him", as he would have said. His reputation as a recruiting officer for Citeaux had spread so far by now that "mothers hid their sons from him and wives their husbands".

We do not know the names of all those whom Bernard had collected at Châtillon but we do know that there were about thirty and that amongst these were his two uncles, all his brothers except Nivard the youngest, and Geoffrey de la Roche, Geoffrey of Aignay, Artauld of Preuilly, Hugh of Mâcon, and Hugh of Montbard. Robert of Châtillon, Bernard's cousin, wanted to join them but was set aside on account of his youth. We shall hear more of him.

After about six months of prayer and solitude at Châtillon Bernard decided that the time had come to set out for Citeaux. They took the road to Dijon and stopped at Fontaines on the way to say good-bye to Tescelin. The old man greeted his sons with great joy and pride, and showed no (apparent) grief at losing them to so high a venture. Yet he would not have been human had he not felt some pangs as he stood at the gate of his castle watching the brave cavalcade of his sons leaving him never to return. His wife was dead and now his sons had left him. Before they departed he gave them one piece of advice. "I know," he said, "how hard it is for you to restrain your high ardour, yet do try to observe some moderation and to avoid dangerous extremes." It was to be some years before Bernard learned to appreciate the quiet wisdom of this advice. As they were riding away they met their youngest brother, Nivard, playing by the side of the road. "Good-bye, Nivard," cried Guy, "you can play on now for you are the heir of all our property." "What!" cried the precocious young urchin, "heaven for you and the world for me? The division is not fair." In a few years he too would leave his father's house and join his brothers.

What sort of life was it that these young noblemen were embracing so blithely? Citeaux, or the New Monastery as it was sometimes called, had been founded by that lovable but enigmatic character St. Robert of Molesme. Stability was not amongst Robert's most outstanding virtues. The Papal Legate, Hugh de Die, refers to his "habitual levity".[1] He had been a monk of St. Michael of Tonnerre before he founded Molesme. The community at Molesme had started off full of enthusiasm but with the accumulation of riches the monks gradually lost their fervour and simplicity. As the need for manual work declined so the Offices in choir became longer and more elaborate, as the riches increased so their life became more soft. Robert lost heart and went off to try the eremitical life. But he soon returned to Molesme and set about trying to restore the primitive simplicity of the life there. Frustrated in his efforts to do this in the year 1098 he again set off, this time taking with him his Prior Alberic, who had suffered much in the cause of reform, the Englishman Stephen Harding, and about nineteen other monks. He settled with his companions on a piece of marshy land given to him by Renard of Béaune and, on 21st March of the same year 1098, he founded there the monastery which was to become the mother house of the whole Cistercian Order. Here he tried to live according to the letter of St. Benedict's Rule. He rejected all that he considered superfluous, everything not explicitly mentioned in the Rule. But he does not appear to have refused endowments. The life he instituted was undoubtedly austere, but it was not austerity for its own sake, it was the austerity that follows as a consequence of seeking God alone, of leading a life of prayer. It was not the vision, it was an effect of the vision. It was not the light, it was the shadow thrown by the light. It is important to remember this when we consider the life of the first Cistercians. The Black Monks were not leading an evil life. Generally speaking the life of the Black Monks was regular, exacting, and in the best sense of the word edifying; but it had lost its primitive simplicity under an accumulation of perhaps rather stultifying traditions. It had become complicated, even perhaps a little pompous, possibly because the monks, preoccupied with a mass of observances and traditions, had lost the contemplative vision which the Rule of St. Benedict, if it does not explicitly mention, at any rate seems to presuppose. The riches with which the faithful had endowed them and sometimes their situation in towns rendered manual work unnecessary and often impracticable, with the result that their life lost the wise harmony of prayer, study, and manual work composed by St. Benedict. It was the achievement of the Cistercians to restore these

[1] "Solita levitas." Early Cistercian historians have quite unscrupulously tampered with the manuscript evidence by changing the word "levitas" into "voluntas".

simple harmonies and to provide for a very short time a haven
where those who wished to seek God alone could live in peace.

St. Robert had never stayed very long anywhere and he did
not stay for more than six months at Citeaux. Under obedience to
the Holy See he returned to Molesme and left St. Alberic in charge
of the new monastery. Alberic seems to have been a rather dour
character. He immediately went much further than his predecessor.
Not content with the situation as he found it he refused all endowments and attempted to maintain his monastery solely by the hard
work of his monks. He also adopted a habit of undyed wool at the
command, so it has been said, of Our Blessed Lady. It could also
have been for motives of economy. By the first measure the community was soon reduced to penury so that the monks began to die
faster than they could be replaced, by the second an impression of
ostentation was created that only served to arouse ridicule amongst
the Black Monks. Finally Alberic died. A man perhaps more
respected than loved. His place was taken by St. Stephen Harding, an Englishman and a native of Dorset.

At one time Stephen had been either a monk or an oblate of
Sherborne but, disgusted for a time with the monastic habit, he set
out for Scotland and afterwards crossed to France where he found
his way to Molesme.[1] Here he returned to the monastic life and
remained to support St. Robert in his reforms. Stephen was a
scholar and an administrator of genius. As soon as he became
Abbot he proved himself every bit as ardent to maintain the high
ideals of his predecessors and took the rather bold step of forbidding
Hugh II, Duke of Burgundy, a loyal and liberal friend of the community, to hold his court at the monastery. But he also proved
himself more realistic by permitting, with prudent safeguards, the
possession of endowments. Henceforth his monks would live just as
austere a life, but they would not die of hunger and cold. Moreover
he inaugurated the immense task of revising the current text of the
Scriptures. A lasting monument to the scholarship of those early
Cistercian Fathers and an irrefutable proof, if proof be needed, of the
esteem in which they held serious intellectual work. The wise and
temperate personality of Stephen has been rather overshadowed by

[1] "Cum seculi urtica solicitaret, pannos illos perosus, primo Scottiam mox Franciam
contendit." William of Malmesbury. There is not the slightest evidence that Stephen
left Sherborne for the sake of study, nor that he ever went to Ireland. See on this the
article by Archdale King in the Downside Review. No. 40. 1941.

the glamour and popularity of his disciple Bernard, and he has received in consequence less attention than he deserves. The rapid spread of the Cistercians and their great popularity were undoubtedly due to the prestige of Bernard, but for the careful organization which made the spread of the Order possible and which gave to it a clear shape and form we have to thank Stephen. The combination of the two characters, of the ardent Burgundian with the cautious Anglo-Saxon, resulted in an Order which retained its primitive spirit for more than one generation, which in the seventeenth century retained enough vigour to put forth the still flourishing Trappist off-shoot, and which still exists in full life today.

"It is not easy," writes Watkin Williams, "for us to estimate in terms of today the discipline which these young nobles accepted as the permanent condition of their lives."[1] It is not indeed, and we must beware of exaggeration. Undoubtedly the life at Citeaux was austere. But the life of all classes in those days was very rough and uncomfortable by modern standards. Many things that would appear to us intolerable, such as the Cistercian custom of sleeping in their workaday habits, were not extraordinary for those times and are indeed common amongst the peasantry of today.

Yet we must not go to the other extreme and under-estimate the physical austerity of the life. Undoubtedly Bernard and his companions would not have found the life there easy in this respect. But for young men used to the rigours of camp life, to giving as well as to receiving hard blows, the physical hardship of the life would not have been intolerable. The real difficulty of the life for these high-spirited and passionate young noblemen, the thing that they must have found all but unbearable, would have been the complete subjection and obedience demanded by the rule and the wearisome tedium of such an existence continuing day after day with little prospect of relief this side of the grave and few if any human consolations. It is the generosity of their whole-hearted submission not merely to the physical but chiefly to the spiritual austerity of the life that should fill us with admiration.

Very little is known of Bernard's time at Citeaux and probably there is little to know. There could have been few ripples in the quiet stream of his life there, little to break the grave monotony of its even course. At first his friends and relations sometimes called

[1] Watkin Williams. *Studies in St. Bernard of Clairvaux.*

and he was shown into the guest-house to meet them. But after a time he found their chatter distracting and adopted the ruse of stuffing his ears with tow so as not to hear what they said. They soon stopped coming.   Perhaps we have a reminiscence of his own trouble over this matter in a letter he wrote many years later to a novice warning him of this very thing.[1]

Bernard had never been very robust. He had always led a rather sheltered and bookish life and, unlike his brothers, he had not been trained to arms. On one occasion, early in his career at Citeaux, he collapsed under the strain of harvesting and had to be given lighter work to do. Mortified at not being able to share in the labours of his brethren he implored God for the strength and skill necessary for a good harvester and, we are told, his prayer was immediately answered so that afterwards he would laughingly boast of his skill in cutting the corn and getting in the harvest. But life at Citeaux was not all manual work; as we have seen they were working on a corrected text of the Vulgate. It is most probable that Bernard acquired his astonishing knowledge of the Scriptures and the Fathers of the Church during his novitiate.

We are told that even when he was a novice Bernard's recollection was so deep that he was afterwards quite unable to say whether the roof of the novices' quarters was vaulted or not or how many windows there were in the sanctuary of the church. This is highly probable, for throughout his active life Bernard always had an exceptional gift of recollection. It is related that he once rode all day by the lake of Geneva without noticing it. Yet no one could be more observant than he when the occasion required. We have only to read his description of the foibles and faults of monks in his treatise on the Degrees of Humility and Pride to realize that there was little in the behaviour of his subjects that he did not notice.

Without any undue drawing on our fancy we can picture Bernard during his novitiate at Citeaux as a fervent and austere young novice throwing himself wholeheartedly into all the rigour of the life; deeply recollected and withdrawn into himself, yet at the same time always smiling and gay.

---

[1] "I advise you, my son, to avoid as far as you can idle talking with guests . . ." Letter 378 (Mabillon 322) to Hugh, a novice, who afterwards became Abbot of Bonneval.

CHAPTER III

WITH the arrival of Bernard and his companions a new era started for Citeaux. The lean years were over, the voice of the turtle dove was heard in the land, and the time for increase had come. It came with a rush. In the year 1113 a foundation was made at La Ferté-sur-Grone in the diocese of Châlon-sur-Saône, and a year later another was made at Pontigny in the diocese of Auxerre of which Hugh of Mâcon became the Abbot. Then in 1115 Stephen decided to make two more foundations, one at Morimond towards the east and another towards the north in the territory of Josbert de la Ferté, and to be the Abbot of this latter he chose Bernard. It caused some remark amongst the older monks that one so young and so frail as Bernard should have been chosen for such a responsible and exacting post, but Stephen had good reasons. Bernard had proved himself a young man of great promise with marked gifts for leadership, moreover he was related by blood to Josbert de la Ferté and many other great families in the neighbourhood. Stephen does not appear to have selected the exact site for Bernard's monastery as he had done for the Abbot of Morimond. The early lives all speak of Bernard setting out to look for a site. Possibly he had merely discussed the matter with Josbert on his way to arrange the affairs of Morimond. It is even possible that Josbert asked for a foundation on his property, believing that it would add prestige to his position, and he would surely have asked after his kinsman Bernard even if he did not ask for him.[1]

In June Bernard set out with a group of twelve monks amongst whom were his brothers Gerard, Guy, and Andrew, his Uncle Gaudry, and probably his cousin Robert of Châtillon. The party passed through Dijon and within a short distance of Langres where they may have broken their journey. The site that Bernard finally chose for his foundation was a valley about seventy miles away from

[1] Vacandard, followed by Watkin Williams, states that Clairvaux was founded at the invitation of Hugh, Count of Champagne. But in *Bernard de Clairvaux*, published by the Trappist-Cistercian Historical Commission (1953), M. Robert Fossier argues convincingly for the view given above, basing his argument partly on the ground that Count Hugh was not favourable to Clairvaux at that time. But see the letter Bernard wrote to the Count when he became a Knight of the Temple, Ep. 32 (Migne 31).

Citeaux in the neighbourhood of Bar-sur-Aube.[1] It was known as the Valley of Absinthe and the early biographers of Bernard have enlarged on its sinister reputation and the evil significance of its name before Bernard and his monks were able to change it from the Valley of Absinthe to the Valley of Light or Clairvaux. They describe it in terms taken from the Life of St. Seine of Châtillon as a lair of robbers and a haunt of wolves and attribute the choice of such an unhealthy situation to Bernard's asceticism. The facts seem to indicate the contrary. Nothing is more probable than that the place was known as the Valley of Absinthe simply for the rather obvious reason that absinthe grew there. Absinthe is a herb with a bitter taste and a not unpleasing smell. It likes sunlight and the shelter of scrub and it does not flourish in dark forests. However strong Bernard's inclination to asceticism it is in the highest degree improbable that he would have jeopardized the whole venture by choosing for it an unsalubrious site. Its beginnings were to be quite difficult enough without adding to them. And it is also most unlikely that an unsalubrious site would have been countenanced by Bernard's brothers and especially by his hard-headed uncle. On more than one occasion Gaudry was to make his views very clear to Bernard. Wolves there may have been. These creatures were common in those days and they would have frequented just such solitary sites as the Cistercians preferred for their foundations. The truth seems to be that Bernard could hardly have found a more suitable site for a foundation within the confines of his kinsman's property. The valley was open to the sun for the greater part of the day, there was ample timber within reach and a stream of running water hard by. Most of his neighbours were his kinsmen and could be relied on to protect both himself and his monks in a crisis.[2]

Very soon after this Bernard set out for Langres to secure confirmation of Josbert's donation by his feudal lord the Count of Champagne and to obtain the abbatial blessing from Joceran the Bishop of Langres. But Joceran was away when Bernard arrived so that he was obliged to go further afield and seek his blessing from the colleague of Joceran, William of Champeaux, the Bishop of

---

[1] Philippe Guignard, archivist of Aube, tried to locate the site of the original monastery about a mile from the traditional place. His theory has been adequately refuted by Vacandard.

[2] The author writes from a personal knowledge of Clairvaux and the neighbourhood.

Châlons-sur-Marne. William of Champeaux was one of the most outstanding Bishops of his time, famous both for his learning and for his sanctity. He had been Archdeacon of Paris and had presided over the Cathedral school when Abelard was attending it. In the year 1108 he founded the Canons of St. Victor and had become one of their number until his appointment to the see of Châlons in the year 1113.

When Bernard arrived at the Bishop's palace he had with him a robust and stalwart monk named Ebald and we are told that there was some speculation amongst the Bishop's entourage as to who was to be the abbot, the robust and mature monk or the frail youth who was with him. But William had no difficulty at all in deciding; he addressed himself immediately to Bernard. A man of God himself, he recognized at once the man of God before him. At their very first meeting mutual respect and admiration united them in a strong friendship which lasted until William's death six years later. From that time Clairvaux became a second home for William and Châlons for the monks of Clairvaux. Bernard certainly could not have had a better friend. William took both him and his monks under his wing and by his timely intervention in the hard times that lay ahead he was able to save Bernard's life when he was dying and with him the existence of the whole community.

It has been a matter of discussion whether Bernard was ordained to the priesthood by William of Champeaux or whether he was already a priest when he came to ask for his abbatial blessing. The sole evidence that we have is William of St. Thierry's biography and this speaks only of the abbatial "ordination" of Bernard and of the question which arose amongst the Bishop's entourage as to who would be the abbot.[1] It certainly seems probable that Bernard was ordained priest before setting out from Citeaux, and there is no evidence to the contrary. This is one of those matters over which scholars love to argue, but it is not one of any importance and adds nothing to our knowledge of Bernard.

When Bernard arrived back at Clairvaux he would probably have found a temporary monastery of wood, simple and austere, already finished or well on the way to being finished. He would also have found a community in very straitened circumstances. There was no

[1] "Cum autem missus noviter Claravallem Bernardus, ordinandus esset in ministerium ad quod assumptus erat . . . cum autem quaereretur quis eorum esset Abbas".

money and little food. Naturally the newly cultivated land had not
yet begun to yield. The monks were living on what they could find,
mostly on wild carrots, berries of various sorts, and very coarse
bread. Bernard was undaunted and urged his monks both by word
and example to yet greater austerities, even beyond those dictated
by the circumstances, remarking that coarse bread and cold water
tasted sweet enough when seasoned by hard work and the love of
God. But the situation did not improve. Even the coarse bread on
which they had been living became scarce, and there was little left
for the monks to eat except what they could find in the woods.
Their habits became threadbare (but they were kept clean because
Bernard hated dirt) and their shoes worn out. The whole venture
seemed to be hanging in the balance and some of the monks were
losing heart. Then one morning just after Mattins in that hour of
hushed quiet which precedes the dawn of another day, Bernard had
a vision. He was walking in the monastery grounds praying God to
vouchsafe some sign of His pleasure, if indeed He was pleased with
their sacrifice, when suddenly he saw the whole valley filled with
men of every age and condition streaming down the glades towards
the monastery. Immensely heartened by this he lost no time in
telling the community, probably during the morning Chapter that
follows Prime. Nevertheless they needed something else to live on
besides berries and visions. His brothers Guy and Gerard told him
that some of the brethren were getting ill, most were losing heart,
and that things could not go on like this; visions or no visions it was
time to go back to Citeaux. We might expect even a Saint to be
perturbed by this situation; things were certainly bad enough to try
the patience of a Saint. Yet what strikes us about Bernard at this
difficult time is his complete composure and serene confidence. It
is not as if he were one of those heavy and phlegmatic men without
nerves and without imagination; on the contrary he shows all the
signs of a highly strung and very imaginative temperament. Such
composure and such serenity in such a character can only come from
on high. Faced with this crisis he showed no sign of panic but
simply went on quietly insisting that what they all wanted more
than any material things was faith, and that if they had faith the
rest would follow. At last all they had left to them was their faith,
but as Bernard foretold their faith was rewarded, not immediately,
not dramatically, but gradually. Every time that the end seemed to
have come at last, Bernard prayed and the way opened up, not for

very far ahead but far enough for the next step. Like a man wrestling with God, Bernard would wring from Providence by his importunity and by his heroic faith always just enough to satisfy the ravenous need of the present moment.

Bernard's Uncle Gaudry was cellarer or bursar at this time and he seems to have been the only hard-headed man of affairs in that ecstatic community. One day he came to Bernard to say that the end had arrived, there was absolutely no money left at all. We can almost hear him say it with that sort of quiet satisfaction with which people sometimes announce a crisis for which they are not responsible and which they have always said would come. "How much money do you want?" asked Bernard. "Eleven pounds," replied Gaudry rather grimly. Eleven pounds in those days was a great deal, not far short of £500 sterling. Bernard prayed and almost at once a good woman arrived with an offering of twelve pounds in thanksgiving for the cure of her husband through Bernard's intercession. On another occasion Bernard told one of his monks to go to market and buy some salt. "That's all very well," said the monk, "but where is the money coming from?" "Money?" replied Bernard. "I have not got any of that and never have had any, what you want in order to buy the salt is faith. Go trusting in God and you will not come back empty-handed." "That's all very well," the monk answered, "but if I go empty-handed I shall surely return empty-handed." However, he went just the same and on the way fell in with a priest to whom he immediately poured out his troubles. The priest was so moved that he gave him all the salt he needed and some money too. On yet another occasion a monk from Clémentinpré paid a visit to Clairvaux and was so edified (or horrified) by the coarse bread he saw the monks eating that he smuggled a loaf back for his own community to see. The result of this was that the community of Clémentinpré sent a whole wagonload of food off to Clairvaux. And so things went on from hand to mouth, from day to day.

During all this time Bernard had not been sparing himself. True he drove his monks hard, but he drove himself even harder. Even while he was a novice he had mortified his sense of taste to such good effect that he seemed quite unaware of what he was eating and drinking. It is recorded that he once drank oil instead of water without noticing the difference. By the Autumn of 1116 he had so undermined his health that a serious gastric complaint, probably an ulcer, made it impossible for him to retain his food. The situation was clearly desperate. Unless something could be done to persuade him to modify his austerities and take reasonable care of himself he could hardly be expected to live through the winter. At last William of Champeaux, having tried in vain to persuade Bernard to a more reasonable frame of mind, took the matter into his own hands and acted with the decision and vigour that the gravity of Bernard's condition demanded. In the September of that year all the abbots of the Order were gathering at Citeaux for their General Chapter. Bernard was of course too weak and ill to think of attending. But William went and, prostrate before the assembled abbots, begged them to give him complete authority over Bernard for one year so that he could make him take reasonable care of his health. The abbots were so touched by the Bishop's humility that they immediately granted him the full authority he asked for. William then made haste back to Clairvaux in order to promulgate his mandate and Bernard, true monk that he was, submitted at once without question. He was immediately relieved of all responsibility and segregated from the common life of the community in a small hut just behind the church. Here he spent a full year trying to recover his health. During this period he was visited by a monk of St. Nicasius of Rheims, William by name, who two years later become Abbot of St. Thierry and, finally, a Cistercian monk at Signy. William of St. Thierry, to call him the name by which he is generally known, became one of Bernard's most devoted and intimate friends, and the author of the first and, in some ways, the most important life of the Saint. The fame of Bernard's sanctity must have been the reason for William's visit, for he tells us that he entered that mean hut where Bernard lay sick with something of the reverence that he approached the altar of God. And he has left us a most precious anecdote of his visit. Apparently the physician who had been chosen to look after Bernard was little better than a conceited boor. William describes how he saw Bernard swallowing at the bidding of this man crude fat and other filthy concoctions with the most complete indifference. And when he asked him how he fared Bernard replied with a gay laugh that he fared splendidly because having hitherto always had reasonable men obedient to him he was now, for his sins, obliged to obey a physician no better than a sort of unreasonable brute. William tells this anecdote probably to show for our edification what Bernard had to suffer at this time, but it is one of the few passages in which his hero comes down from the pedestal on which he places him and flashes into life.[1]

After his year of isolation Bernard returned to community life and took up again the office which he had laid down. But it is to be feared that his health was little improved. He still found it almost impossible to retain food. A place had to be made next to him in choir where he could void his undigested food and eventually he became so bad that he was forced once more to withdraw himself, at any rate to a certain extent, from the common life of his community. William of St. Thierry speaks of a stream of phlegm flowing from his mouth. At last the end seemed near. Bernard lay on his bed sick and dying. His monks were gathered round him. Finally, when his suffering had become almost unendurable, he told one of his brethren who stood by to go at once to the oratory to pray for him. Protesting that his prayers would not be of much use the monk went as he was told and visited in turn the altars of Our Blessed Lady, St. Laurence and St. Benedict. At the same moment Bernard clearly beheld standing over him Our Blessed Lady herself accompanied by the two other Saints to whom the monk had prayed. He saw them lay their hands upon him and from that moment his pains left him. The prayers of an obedient monk had achieved what the foresight and devotion of the great William of Champeaux had failed to do; Bernard was restored to health.

In the meantime Bernard's reputation as a man of God, even as a thaumaturgist, was spreading all over the countryside. Whenever he was fit to do so he appears to have travelled about the neighbourhood preaching, and he had not lost any of his old power to persuade and influence others. As early as 1116 after a sermon at Châlons he brought back with him to Clairvaux a group of noble youths, the pupils of Stephen of Vitry. A little later their master Stephen also knocked on the door of Clairvaux. "This man has come alone and he will depart alone," declared Bernard in his prophetic role. Nevertheless he allowed him to try the life. But the

---

[1] Surely Fossier and other authorities are mistaken when they say that this visit took place in the year 1118. William found Bernard segregated in the hut and we know he remained there only for a year. But this must have been, on the evidence of William himself, from immediately after William of Champeaux had appealed to the Chapter in 1116 until the Autumn of the year 1117. Another point which seems to have escaped the notice of Bernard's modern biographers is that William seems to imply that he was himself an abbot when he visited Bernard ("cum ibi cum quodam *abbate altero* visitarem . . .") but we know that William did not become Abbot of St. Thierry until 1119. See *Guillaume de St. Thierry*, J. M. Dechanet.

event proved the truth of his prophecy, for, while all the young noblemen persevered, Stephen having put his hand to the plough turned back and left Clairvaux. One wonders if he had heard of Bernard's prophecy while he was there. It could not have been a very encouraging start for him.

The miracles of Bernard were hardly less embarrassing to himself and his community than they are to some of us. His uncle Gaudry seems to have been highly suspicious of them. More than once he nearly reduced Bernard to tears by telling him that for a man like him to attempt to do miracles was sheer presumption, and that at any rate there was nothing in them. But one day Gaudry himself fell seriously ill and at once sent for Bernard and begged him to bless and cure him. "Sorry, my dear Uncle," said Bernard smiling, "I fear I can't do that, it would be sheer presumption for me to attempt any such thing." Whereupon Gaudry pleaded that he had only been trying to save his nephew from pride, that he had not really meant what he had said about his miracles. In the end Bernard blessed him and cured him both of his illness and of scoffing at his miracles. On another occasion William of St. Thierry fell ill and Bernard, who was none too well himself at the time, sent him a message by his brother Gerard asking him to come to Clairvaux to keep him company and promising that he would either get quite well there or die. The good William tells us that he was both delighted and flattered by the invitation and could hardly make up his mind whether it would be better to live or to die in that holy man's company. He gives us a charming picture of himself and Bernard, both sick men, chatting together of spiritual things in the infirmary or whatever did service as an infirmary at Clairvaux. William recovered from his illness and by the Saturday before Septuagesima his health was so far restored that, although still a little weak, he began to think it was time for him to return to his monastery. However Bernard would not hear of his leaving Clairvaux just yet. He persuaded him to stay on until the beginning of Lent and one feels that he did not have much difficulty in doing so. But William insisted that if he was to stay on he should at least begin again to abstain from meat. Bernard was strongly opposed to this and William stubbornly determined on it. And so they parted for the night, William to his bed and Bernard to Compline. They had obviously quarrelled as even holy men will. That night poor William's illness returned worse than ever. He was seized with the most excruciating pains and as he tossed and turned on his bed he began to wonder if he would ever live to see the dawn and talk to Bernard again. But dawn came at last and with the dawn came Bernard looking rather severe. "Well," he said, "what will you have to eat now?" Then poor William realized that his illness had returned in order to punish him for his obstinacy of the night before and meekly replied that he would eat whatever he was given. Whereupon Bernard broke into one of his gay laughs and assured him that he would not die and that he would send up for him a good helping of meat. "And," says William, "I became immediately as well as ever except for feeling a little weak owing to my sleepless night." On the whole one feels that Bernard had used his powers a little unfairly on this occasion. William was not one of his monks and was in no way obliged to obey him.

Bernard had always been on the best of terms with his young sister Hombeline. But she did not follow him into religion, instead she married and settled down to bring up her family. One day in the year 1122 she thought that she would like to visit her brothers and especially her favourite Bernard. Wishing to do them honour she appeared at the gates of Clairvaux magnificently arrayed and with a huge retinue of servants. But to her dismay Bernard, instead of hurrying to meet her as she had been confident he would, sent a curt message by their brother Andrew, who was the monastery porter at the time, that he would not see her. Andrew improved the situation by saying that she was no better than a dressed-up baggage, a bait of the devil to lure men to destruction, and concluded by expressing the pious and brotherly wish that she was ashamed of herself. At this poor Hombeline burst into tears and sent Andrew back to beg Bernard to come to her if not as his sister at any rate as a poor sinner for whom Christ had died. In answer to this appeal Bernard came and told her that if she were really repentant she should put away her worldliness and try to live with her husband as their mother had lived with Tescelin. After this Hombeline returned home a different woman. She laid aside her finery and devoted herself to a life of penance and good works. After two years of this her husband died and left her free to enter a convent at Jully where she persevered in the life of prayer she had begun in the world and proved herself in every way worthy of her holy brothers.

There can be little doubt that in the early years at Clairvaux Bernard had been led by his ardent nature to extremes that nobody could consider wise or discreet, little doubt but that he drove both himself and his monks too hard. It was a pity in some respects that he had been quite unable to follow his father's advice to him when he left Fontaines. Yet had he been able to do so he would never have been the great and ardent lover that he was. It must not be forgotten that he was both young in years and young in religion when he became Abbot of Clairvaux, barely twenty-five years old! At that age every young man with anything to him is prone to extremes, "it is the hot condition of their blood," and this is especially true of "Sons of Thunder" like Bernard. Of such stuff Saints are made, but the Lord preserve us from them when they are in the making! Tolerance and gentleness came to him with years and experience and the tears that years and experience bring. Soon he would be writing to the parents of a young monk at Clairvaux, "Do not worry about the frail health of your son, for I shall look after him like a father and he shall be for me a son. I will be to him both a father and a mother, both a brother and a sister, and I will so temper and arrange all things for him that his soul may profit without his body suffering." And to one of his monks whom he had sent to be abbot of the foundation at Foigny he wrote: "You must understand that you are especially the abbot of the sad, faint-hearted, and discontented amongst your flock. You were given to them as abbot not to be comforted but to comfort because you were the strongest of them all and, by God's grace, able to comfort them all without needing to be comforted by any."[1] This is a very different Bernard from the one who only a few years before told his novices at Clairvaux that they must leave their bodies outside the gates of the monastery and was astonished to discover that all his monks were not saints.

[1] Ep. 112 (Migne 110) and Ep. 76 (Migne 73).

CHAPTER IV

In the midst of all the worries and troubles of the early years at Clairvaux Bernard was dealt a sharp and stinging blow from a quarter whence he would least have expected it. During his absence from Clairvaux, the Grand Prior of Cluny came and snatched away Robert of Châtillon. The story behind this rather unpleasant incident is long and complicated and there is something to be said on both sides.

Very soon after the foundation of Clairvaux the Cistercian movement began to sweep the world like a tornado and trouble with unwelcome dreams the fat slumbers of the old Benedictine houses. Soon the foundations sent out from Citeaux were themselves making other foundations; Clairvaux was no exception; neither the illness of Bernard nor the desperate economic situation could hinder her increase. The year 1118 saw her first foundation at Troisfontaines in the Duchy of Bar and the next year yet another, this time at Fontenay about four miles from Montbard. And so the increase went on until the whole of Western Europe was peopled by Cistercian monks and men began saying that the whole world was becoming Cistercian. By the time of Bernard's death in 1153 Clairvaux alone had no less than sixty-five daughter houses, thirty-eight in France, eight in Spain, six in England, four in Italy, three in Portugal, two in Belgium, two in Sweden, one in Sardinia, and one in Sicily.

In the same year as the foundation at Fontenay Stephen Harding settled the distinctive character of the Order and consolidated its gains by a famous document known to the world as the Carta Caritatis. This document assigned Citeaux as the mother house of the Order, constituted the yearly General Chapter of abbots as the governing body, and defined the limits of the abbot's authority in his own house. It established uniformity of observance and liturgy throughout and provided for the curbing of abuses and irregularity by an annual visitation of all the houses. The Carta Caritatis was undoubtedly conceived, planned and composed by Stephen Harding and it is unquestionably a masterpiece of monastic legislation; but it would not be accurate to describe it as something quite new, it was rather a codification of ideas that had been current for some time. Much of it had already been observed at Vallombrosa since the latter half of the preceding century. Nevertheless by the application of the ideas it embodies within the framework of the old monastic tradition Stephen Harding achieved something both original and revolutionary.[1] Indeed it might perhaps be more true to describe the Cistercian movement as a revolution rather than a reform, something of a social revolution in a monastic context.

The Benedictines, or Black Monks as they were called to distinguish them from the Cistercians who wore white habits, had not been unfavourable to the Cistercians in their early days of poverty and obscurity and on more than one occasion they came to the rescue of Clairvaux with considerable gifts of food and money. But it would be asking far too much of human nature to expect them to view the sudden rise to fame and favour of this *parvenu* Order with equanimity. The very claim of the Cistercians to follow perfectly the Rule of St. Benedict could not but seem invidious to the Benedictines. Until the rise of the Cistercians to popularity the Black Monks and especially the congregation of Cluny had held an acknowledged place in the esteem of Christendom. The Church of Cluny was one of the wonders of the world and her interpretation of the Rule was regarded as the only practical one for the majority of men. Her way of life was acknowledged by Bernard himself as "honourable, beautiful for its chastity, famous for its discretion, sanctioned by the Fathers, inspired by the Holy Spirit, and well fitted to save souls".[2] In saying this Bernard was only expressing the general opinion of his day. But by the twelfth century there was a new spirit abroad, men were beginning to find the great traditions of Cluny and the endless Offices in choir rather ponderous and wearisome; they wanted something simpler and less ritualistic, they wanted, as it

[1] See *Bernard de Clairvaux. Commission de Histoire de l'Ordre de Citeaux*, p. 105.

In an order that since the Reformation and even before then has been dominated largely by the French the Englishman Stephen Harding has received less than his due. It is furthermore interesting to speculate on how far Bernard and Stephen agreed in their views on the Cistercian life. It would be quite contrary to all we know of human nature and of Bernard's temperament if there had never been any vigorous difference of opinion between two men so very different. But there is no real evidence of any conflict; on the other hand we can be quite sure that if there had been any evidence it would have been suppressed. We have the quarrel between St. Basil and his friend St. Gregory to remind us that even Saints do not always live in brotherly concord, we also have Bernard's opinion of St. William of York: "a man rotten from the soles of his feet to the crown of his head"!

[2] Apol., ch. 2.

were, to escape into the open air. The great success of the Cistercians was partly due to their filling this newly-felt need and also to the fact that whilst the ordinary men and women of the day were finding it increasingly difficult to understand the rather stately life of the Black Monks the quite obvious asceticism and poverty of the Cistercians made an instant appeal which no one could fail to appreciate and admire. When the poor saw rich and noble young men freely and gaily embracing a way of life quite as poor and a great deal harder than theirs, they felt their own life to be exalted and ennobled. But no one could expect the Black Monks to take this view; they believed that their reputation had been filched and their thunder stolen by a body of men who were little better than adventurers. "Who can see without repining," wrote Peter the Venerable Abbot of Cluny and one of Bernard's most devoted friends, "these newcomers preferred to us and their way of life praised at the expense of ours." If things had gone no further than this, little harm would have been done, but feelings began to run high and there were regrettable incidents. "The different colour of your habit," wrote Peter the Venerable again, "is a source of discord. For, as everyone is aware and as I have repeatedly seen myself, the Black Monk looks down his nose when he sees a White Monk, and a White Monk turns his back when he sees a Black Monk coming." It is tempting to ask what the White Monks were doing wandering about outside their cloisters; the Carthusians managed to keep within theirs; "The White Monks are always on the road," was a familiar gibe of the Black Monks.[1] But however natural and even reasonable the complaints of the Black Monks may have been, however supercilious the White Monks may have seemed, there was no excuse whatsoever for the Grand Prior of Cluny abducting one of the young monks of Clairvaux behind Bernard's back, and yet this is precisely what he did.

　　Robert of Châtillon was the cousin of Bernard, being the son of Otho of Châtillon and Diana the younger daughter of Robert of Montbard. When he was still quite a child his parents promised him to Cluny, but when he was old enough to make up his own mind he chose to follow his illustrious kinsman into the Cistercian Order. At first the Cistercians refused to accept him on the grounds of his youth and advised him to wait and apply again, but Robert would take no refusal and continued to pester the Abbot of Citeaux

[1] "Monachi grisei semper vagantur."

with tears in his eyes until at length permission was granted for him to enter the Order, although it is not certain whether he entered at Citeaux and followed Bernard to Clairvaux or entered directly at Clairvaux. At first all went well and Robert was a model of observance, but no sooner had the novelty of the life begun to wear off than his thoughts began to wander to Cluny and the more benign life to be found there. Very soon the insidious thought became parent to the perilous doubt as to whether he did not in fact belong to Cluny by virtue of his oblation and had not done wrong in joining the Cistercians. It was not long before Pons, the Abbot of Cluny, heard rumours of this, perhaps Robert managed to get a message to him. But the Abbot took no immediate action, he awaited his opportunity, and soon this came in the absence of Bernard on one of his missions. As soon as he heard of this Abbot Pons took immediate action by sending to Clairvaux the Grand Prior of Cluny, Bernard de Brancion. This Bernard de Brancion was a very grand gentleman indeed, both on account of his office and of his noble birth, and he arrived at Clairvaux in state. The poor monks seem to have been impressed and not a little flattered by the visit of such an important personage, and when he declared that he had come to confirm Robert in his vocation they made no difficulty at all in admitting him, with the result that he confirmed Robert in his vocation to such good effect that he was able to take him away to Cluny when he left. When Robert arrived at Cluny he was welcomed by the Abbot and community, in the words of Watkin Williams, "like a child rescued from the gypsies". They washed and scrubbed him, clothed him in a clean habit, and allotted him a position in the community far above his contemporaries. So as to spike Bernard's guns and allay any scruple of Robert's they sent off post haste to Rome for a rescript confirming their triumph and Robert's downfall on the pretext of his oblation to Cluny by his parents.

But however plausible the plea of Cluny that Robert belonged to them by reason of his oblation, it is difficult to see how anyone could have condoned the action of Abbot Pons in snatching him away from Clairvaux behind Bernard's back, amounting as it did to kidnapping the boy. Yet it must not be regarded as an isolated event, it was rather an incident in the growing rivalry between the two Orders of monks for which doubtless both must take their share of blame and which no one regretted more than Bernard.[1]

[1] Apol., ch. 5.

When Bernard returned to Clairvaux and found his young kinsman had been carried off to Cluny he was prostrated with grief yet unable to do anything or take any effective action in view of the rescript obtained by Cluny from Rome. It is not known how long he waited before taking any action, but in writing to Jorannus, Abbot of St. Nicasius of Rheims, he says: "When one of my own monks, not only a professed religious but also a kinsman of mine, was received and kept at Cluny against my will, I was certainly upset but I held my peace and prayed to God for those who had carried him off that they might return him, and for him that he might come back of his own free will," and Geoffrey of Auxerre says that he waited several years.[1]

It cannot have been easy for a tempestuous nature like Bernard's to keep silent and inactive in the face of such a flagrant act of injustice against himself and his monastery. At last he could restrain himself no longer and poured out his pent-up sorrow in a famous letter addressed to Robert. The circumstances under which this letter was written were peculiar. Bernard had retired with his secretary to a remote part of the enclosure so that he could dictate it without interruption, but hardly had he begun than heavy rain started to fall. When his secretary (who tells the story himself) tried to cover up the parchment and take shelter Bernard, whose grief would brook no delay, cried out: "Write on, this is the work of God!" and although the rain fell fast not one drop touched the parchment. He begins the letter by saying that he had waited before writing in the hope that Robert might repent and return to Clairvaux of his own free will, and then he proceeds to blame himself for having driven the boy away by his severity but adds, "You need have no fear that in future you will have anything to complain of from me because even while you are far away I have cast myself at your feet, humbled myself before you, and assured you of my love." Very touching indeed and no doubt the right approach to a young man whose head has been turned by adulation, and also from all that we know of Bernard in those early days it is not unlikely that he had been too severe on the boy. When he comes to describe the action of the Grand Prior of Cluny the indignation of Bernard boils

---

[1] Ep. 33 (Migne 32). If Mabillon is correct in his dating of this letter of Jorannus 1120, he is surely wrong in saying that Bernard wrote his appeal to Robert in 1119 for we know both from Bernard himself and from what Geoffrey of Auxerre tells us that he waited for some time before writing it.

over in a cascade of invective: "Outwardly he came in sheep's clothing, but underneath a ravening wolf was concealed. Alas! the shepherds were deceived by this semblance to a sheep and admitted him to the fold. . . . Once there he commended feasting and condemned fasting, called voluntary poverty wretchedness and poured scorn upon our fasts, vigils, silence, and manual labour. He called sloth contemplation, and gluttony, chattering and intemperance he commended as discretion."

Bernard could not have meant all this to be taken *au pied de la lettre* for it is very hard to believe that the Grand Prior of Cluny spoke in quite this way and if Bernard was absent how did he know what the Grand Prior had said? It is not likely that he would have so far discarded his sheep's clothing as to say all this before the community; if he had said it at all he would have done so in private to Robert. "In the meantime," Bernard continues, "representations were made at Rome. The Pope himself was cajoled. To make certain of his consent, it was suggested to him that this youth while yet a child had been offered to Cluny by his parents. There was no one present to refute this nor was it anticipated that there would be. Judgement was pronounced on the case in the absence of the judged. This gist of the rescript, the sum of the judgement, the whole significance of the suit, was nothing more than that the robbers could keep their spoils and that those who lost thereby should be made to keep silent. And all this that a soul for whom Christ died should be lost in order to satisfy Cluny." Then with a characteristic gesture Bernard appeals from Rome to the Judgement-seat of God: "To your judgement-seat, Lord Jesu, I appeal . . ." and a very moving appeal it is.

When Bernard deals with the case in dispute he lays aside rhetoric and argues with all the force and vigour of which he is master that in fact no formal oblation of the child had ever been made and that even if it had, "Which has the most force: the vow a father makes on behalf of his son, or the vow a son makes on his own behalf, especially when it is a vow to do something better; a vow made for a child when it is too young to know anything about it, or the vow he makes afterwards when he realizes and understands what he is doing?" After this Bernard turns to Robert and addresses him: "You foolish boy! Who has bewitched you to break the vows your lips have uttered? Does salvation depend on soft raiment and high living rather than on frugal fare and moderate clothing? White bread, honey wine and pittances, benefit the body but not the soul. The soul is not fattened out of frying-pans! Arise, soldier of Christ, I say, arise! Shake off the dust and return to battle. You will fight more valiantly after your flight and you will conquer more gloriously." It is impossible to do justice to this fine letter in mere extracts. It has all Bernard's characteristic felicities of style as well as many of his weaknesses. Sometimes he appears to mistake rhetoric for arguments but the rhetoric is always sincere, the self-expression of an intensely emotional and sensitive nature, and when he lays aside rhetoric and begins to argue we see him at his best. No one in his day had such a power of pointed and vigorous argument or, one must say, of invective.

And what happened to the wretched Robert? It is highly unlikely that he ever received the letter. Yet in the end he did return to Clairvaux although not until some ten years later and, in the year 1136, Bernard made him Abbot of Noirlac in the diocese of Bourges.

CHAPTER V

THE abduction of Robert did not serve at all to establish good relations between Cluny and the Cistercians. Nevertheless three years later things took a turn for the better when Abbot Pons de Melgueil died and was succeeded by Peter de Montbossier, better known as Peter the Venerable: a title no man deserved better than he. In contrast to the worldly Abbot Pons, Peter was a man of deep spiritual life, great learning, and careful prudence; he was also a man of peace and soon became one of Bernard's most devoted friends. It was Peter who made the first approach, and the letter he wrote to Bernard is of the greatest historical interest. He begins by saying that although they had never met he had learned to love Bernard from his reputation. He then goes on to say that he was worried by the accusations that certain Cistercians were making against Cluny and that he was writing them all in a letter together with the answers of the monks of Cluny so that he might have Bernard's opinion on it all, for he well knew him to be a very learned and spiritual man. Adopting the expedient of putting the replies of Cluny to the Cistercian criticisms into the mouth of an anonymous monk of his congregation, Peter is, however, careful to explain that "praeter austeritatem verborum", they are nevertheless his own. This letter is an immensely long document running into more than forty columns of Migne and it is quite impossible to quote the whole of it. But it is too important an element in the controversy between the Black Monks and the Cistercians to pass over without attempting to give some idea of its contents.

The anonymous monk of Cluny starts off his defence by carrying war into the Cistercian camp. "Behold a new race of Pharisees has come amongst us!" he says. "They set themselves up above everyone else saying, as the Prophet foretold they would say: 'Touch me not for I am clean.' Tell us, O holy men, the only true monks in the world, why this habit of so unusual a colour? Why alone amongst all the monks of the world do you dare to appear clothed in white? No doubt at all that you reject the black habit which our fathers chose for the sake of humility because you reject their humility and believe yourselves better than anyone else. You despise the colour

49

suited to a humble condition and choose to wear white which we read in the Scriptures symbolizes joy and glory." Then he answers the accusation of the Cistercians that the monks of Cluny receive novices too easily: "You accuse us of receiving novices without first trying them, but in doing this we only follow the rule which all men are bound to follow: 'All that the Father has entrusted to me will come to me, and him who comes to me I will not cast out.' We should certainly not be faithful to this rule if we refused to accept those who were inspired by the Father to come to the Father 'for no one cometh to me unless the Father, who sent me, draw him'. It is true that not only do we receive those who come but also invite those who would not do so otherwise according to the words, 'Come unto me all ye who labour and are heavily burdened and I will refresh you'. In receiving those who come to us we try to make charity our rule, and we do not believe that by doing this we are breaking the Rule of St. Benedict. Sometimes it happens that those who have submitted themselves to the yoke after a little time are troubled and oppressed by temptations and but for their vows would return to the filth that they have left. And if occasionally they do presume to do this and afterwards, fearful for their salvation, return to the fold because they know not how else they can save their souls, we receive them back. And St. Benedict whom you quote against us we in turn quote against you saying: 'Let the Abbot so temper and arrange all things that souls may be saved'."

"You ask us by what authority we defend our use of furs and coverings since there is nothing about them in the Rule. But we ask you by what authority you try to deprive us of them. And as you cannot tell us this we will give you our reasons for using them: 'Let clothes,' says the Rule, 'be given to the brethren, suitable for the place and climate in which they live. In cold regions more will be required, in hot less' and he leaves the decision to the Abbot. In allotting these extra clothes we act both according to the Rule and according to the Acts of the Apostles where we read: 'Each could have what share of the common property he needed'."

"Now we come to the two dishes of cooked food which you mention and to the share of bread and wine. Let us see what the Rule has to say about this. 'Let one pound of bread,' it says, 'suffice for the day, whether there be but one meal or both dinner and supper. If they are to sup, let a third part of the pound be kept back by the cellarer and given to the brethren for supper.' Now you have your opportunity, you who scheme to trip us up with trifles and argue about details. You have caught us out, arise then and attack us! If some of us should exceed our allowance of bread, if some of us should eat rather more than the allotted third of a pound in the evening, clearly we are condemned by God, excluded for ever from Paradise, and confined to the depths of hell as perjurers who have broken their vows. But what does the Rule say? 'If,' it says, 'their work has been greater than usual, it shall be within the power of the Abbot, if he deems it expedient, to make some addition to the allowance of food, providing that excess be before all things avoided so that no monk shall suffer from surfeiting.' What else does St. Benedict mean by this than to provide for necessity while cutting off excess and to leave the decision to the Abbot?"

It will be clear to the reader that the Cistercians and the monks of Cluny are arguing from two completely different points of view. The Cistercian is taking the line that nothing is justified beyond a literal interpretation of the Rule of St. Benedict. Such an attitude is perfectly permissible and, for a certain type, it is the only possible; but it could never be more. In fact it is not even wholly practical in every respect owing to the silence of the Rule on certain matters and also owing to the changes in the world since the Rule was written, and this the Cistercians were very soon to find out for themselves. On the other hand the monks of Cluny by defending their interpretation of the rule on the grounds of development open the door wide for abuse and corruption. If everything is to be left completely to the discretion of the Abbot, regardless of the explicit injunctions of the Rule, then the whole of the life is at the mercy of one man. To excuse the use of furs on the basis of the passage quoted from the Rule may be legitimate, but to excuse the profession of novices without first trying them to see if they are truly seeking God, on the grounds of charity but in the teeth of the explicit instructions of the Rule, is ultimately to change the very nature of the life envisaged by St. Benedict, open the door to every sort of abuse, and on the long view to act contrary to the truest charity. Large numbers even with the best will in the world cannot live as monks, and to profess such men would in the end mean pulling down the whole tenor of the life to their level. On the other hand the way of life at Cluny, apart from the abuses and corruptions that had crept in, was based on a perfectly legitimate interpretation of the Rule and was the only one possible for the majority of men who were truly called to seek God in the cloister. There was certainly room in the Church for both the Cistercian and the Cluniac way of life, and there still is.

But however clearly men like Peter the Venerable and Bernard might understand this and be able to respect the different views of each other, it is too much to expect such an objective outlook from lesser men. It would be idle to look from the majority of monks for the wide horizons and profound charity of men like Peter the Venerable and Bernard: most men, even when they are monks, are moved by more primitive emotions. There is no doubt that certain Cistercians were critical and supercilious towards their brother Black Monks, Bernard admits as much, but it cannot be denied that the Black Monks were the more aggressive, and it was Bernard whom they made the target of their attacks, it was he whom they cited as their main adversary. This is not surprising, for by his eloquence and dominating character he had acquired for himself the position of spokesman and main protagonist of the Cistercian reform. At length matters came to such a pass that Bernard was approached by two friends, William of St. Thierry and a certain Canon Oger, and urged to write something in his own defence and also to draw attention to some abuses prevalent at Cluny. Bernard was most unwilling to do any such thing for fear of making matters worse, and also he did not wish to fall into the same fault as his adversaries and many monks of his own Order by criticizing a way of life that was not his own, but in the end he decided that he could not allow things to go on as they were without saying something in defence of himself and his Order. Thus we have the famous Apologia of Bernard which rattled through the cloisters of Europe like a cartload of bricks.

In order fully to appreciate Bernard's Apologia we must first try to understand his point of view when he wrote it. He was torn in two ways: his respect for Cluny was sincere and there is no doubt that he was completely truthful in saying that he himself would have become a monk at Cluny had he thought he could have saved his soul there, but on the other hand the external pomp and ceremony of the life repelled him. Some men, he would have said, can save their souls at Cluny; but he had not the slightest doubt that his own Order was both a more perfect and a more certain way to salvation. If a friend of his chose to enter Cluny, he would not condemn him; but if that friend had first decided to become a

Cistercian, then the situation would be different and Bernard would have considered that he had failed to respond to God's grace for, in his view, such a man would have rejected the better for the lesser goal and that, however well he might stand before men, in God's eyes he would be a backslider. In support of this view Bernard would have quoted St. Gregory (as indeed he does under similar circumstances) saying that if a man should choose the highest and then look back and choose a lesser good, then, however well he may seem to be doing, before God who searches the heart he would have fallen away. As for the various mitigations and even luxuries that had been introduced into certain houses of Black Monks, Bernard would have none of them, in his view they were utterly unwarranted. Nevertheless we must bear in mind that the abuses and luxuries pilloried by Bernard were not prevalent in every house of Black Monks or cell of Cluny, that he dedicated the Apologia to William of St. Thierry who was a Black Monk, and that it was the same William of St. Thierry who persuaded him to write it and also apparently suggested the main lines on which he should direct his attack. Although it is only Bernard's trenchant and often witty criticisms of the life at Cluny and other houses of Black Monks that are generally quoted, yet a good half of the whole Apologia is devoted to praising the ideals of Cluny and castigating in words every bit as severe as those he uses against the Black Monks, his own Cistercians who, in the spirit of the Pharisees, proudly and self-righteously ridiculed their brother monks of a different Order.

In a short letter to William of St. Thierry which prefaces his Apologia Bernard says: "I willingly undertake the task you have placed on me of removing scandal from the Kingdom of God. Affectionately reading and re-reading that most dear letter of yours I understand that you wish me to answer those who complain that I slander the Order of Cluny so that they may see that this is not true and that they have formed or tried to form a wrong opinion of me. But if after answering them I begin to criticize their superfluous clothes and food and other things as you suggest, I should then seem to contradict myself, and I do not see how I can do it without giving scandal. . . ." However, he soon found out how to do it effectively if not without giving scandal and the result was what in modern jargon we call a rocket.

He starts off by praising Cluny and then asks: "How can I, the most miserable of men 'living in deserts, in rock-fastnesses, and in caves in the ground' be said to judge the world, and what would be more intolerable than to criticize the most glorious Order of Cluny and impudently slander the holy men who live in it such praiseworthy lives? If, puffed up with my own self-esteem like the Pharisees, I despise other men and (what is worse) men better than myself, what does all my austerity profit me? Surely I could find an easier way to hell!" Then rounding on the monks of his own Order who had been ridiculing other monks he says: "Now I come to those of my own Order who contrary to the words 'Judge not before the time . . .' are said to calumniate other Orders and make their own way of life the only norm of righteousness. These men, if there are any, do not belong to us, nor in fact to any Order, since although they live in an orderly way they make themselves citizens of Babylon by their pride, nay rather they are the sons of darkness and of hell itself. . . ." Having thus cleared himself and declared his esteem for the ideals of Cluny Bernard then, rather reluctantly, turns to the abuses and corruptions of the Black Monks: "I cannot think how such intemperance in food and drink, in dress and bed-clothes, in equipages and buildings, ever arose amongst monks. Matters have come to such a pass that where these excesses flourish most, there the Order is said to be in a better state and religion prospering. Frugality is deemed to be mean; sobriety is called austerity; and silence is considered melancholy; but dissipation is regarded as discretion; laughter as holy joy; effeminate clothes and fine equipages as honourable; elaborate bed-coverings as cleanliness. . . . At table one course follows another. In the place of flesh-meat great fish are provided. When you are satisfied with one course, if you begin on the next you feel as if you had not eaten a thing for the skill of the cooks is so great that no matter how many different dishes appear you are still able to eat more. Variety dispels all sense of repletion and the stomach is filled without your knowing it." This is certainly a vivid picture of high living at monastic tables and no doubt it has not suffered any loss of colour in the telling. We must once more remind ourselves that not all Black Monks lived like this; there were many monasteries where even Bernard would find nothing to criticize. But highly coloured as Bernard's description may be, there can be little doubt that it is substantially accurate. Peter the Venerable himself criticizes the excesses of some of the monasteries under his jurisdiction in words hardly less strong than Bernard's.

After speaking his mind on the luxurious food served in the refectories of the Black Monks, Bernard then turns on the expensive clothes worn by some of the abbots and on the great state which they kept. It all makes good reading but it had all been said before, although perhaps not so well; it is when deploring the great monastic buildings and elaborate churches that Bernard strikes a more original note: "But these matters are small things," he says, referring to what has gone before, "I come to greater abuses. Of the enormous size of their oratories, their great height, their superfluous breadth, their sumptuous polished marbles and curious paintings which, while they distract the eye, impede the recollection of those who should be praying, I have nothing to say. For me it all savours of the worship of the Jews in the Temple, but let it be, I assume it is all for the honour and glory of God." Clearly Bernard does not approve of these great monastic churches and is ill at ease in them. But he is too intelligent not to realize that great Abbeys like Cluny with an enormous choir of monks and pilgrims from every part of Europe needed larger churches than comparatively small and unknown houses. Some Cistercian communities were to build churches that for size would rival those of the Black Monks, and it would not be very long before the monks of Clairvaux itself would rebuild their monastery and church on a grander scale.[1] But Bernard feels on safer ground when he comes to the ornaments of monastic churches: "A monk myself, I will ask you my brother monks what a pagan poet asked his fellow pagans: 'tell me, ye priests of God, to what purpose the gold in your holy places?' And I say: Tell me, poor men, (if indeed you are poor), what is the gold doing in your holy places? We monks are differently situated to bishops; they have a duty to their people not all of whom are spiritual, and they must try to stir up their devotion by material things. But whose devotion do we hope to stir up by ornaments of gold and silver, we who have left the world and every thing precious and splendid?" and he goes on in well known and too often quoted words to denounce the gorgeous ornaments and carvings in some of the greater houses of Black Monks.

The Cistercian and the Cluniac attitude towards ecclesiastical

[1] Nowadays even some Trappist oratories rival parish churches for the quantity of their bondieuserie. If we want to see a Cistercian oratory as it was at the height of the Order's glory we must visit Fontenay in Burgundy, or the modern monastery at Mount St. Bernard in Leicestershire.

architecture and the adornment of Churches represent two different
and quite legitimate ideals, it might even be said two quite different
vocations. The attitude of Cluny and of the majority of men and
women in those days if not in ours was that nothing is too good or
too valuable for the worship of God and the glory of his house.
In the times of which we write men and women of all classes gave
the best they could afford for this purpose, and they gave spon-
taneously and joyously. In passing it might be said that nowadays
we are inclined to want magnificence without the cost and in consequence our churches are full of sham gold, sham gems, and sham
statues of plaster imitating wood or stone. It was otherwise in the
days of faith when men and women poured out their gold and
jewels for the glory of God's house. A classical example of this is
the great Suger, Abbot of the royal Abbey of St. Denis. He was a
councillor of the King and a great feudal lord, and he must have been
in Bernard's mind when he inveighed against the proud equipages
of some Benedictine abbots and the lordly state in which they lived.
He was also one of the abbots who were smitten to the heart by the
flaming words of the Apologia. He promptly reformed his monks,
cutting off all superfluities and, what is more, he also reformed his
own way of life. He gave up his fine horses and sumptuous liveries
and he left his enormous house, the abbot's lodging, for a cell so
small that "men were amazed and filled with wonder". Yet his love
of gorgeous churches and a splendid ceremonial did not abate one
bit; his undoubtedly sincere conversion did not change him at all in
this respect; he continued to adorn his great church with every sort
of precious ornament until it glowed like the courts of Heaven.
Indeed it was just this that he had in mind, for he was a man obsessed
by the symbolism of the Old Testament and all ornaments, carvings,
and sculpture with which he filled his church were meant to speak
to hearts not only of the heavenly Jerusalem described in the
Apocalypse but also, by symbols and allegory, of the union of the
Old and New Testaments. Just at the time of his conversion he had
caused to be made a huge crucifix of gilded bronze and enriched by
priceless jewels. There were rubies for the wounds in Christ's hands
and feet and the cross itself was covered with pearls of great size and
rarity. Around the base of this cross, in bas-relief of gold, all the
story of Christ's death and passion was told in the allegories of the
Old Testament. What is most interesting and suggestive is that
the Abbot of Citeaux (not, however, of Clairvaux) contributed

some great pearls for this crucifix and that it was solemnly blessed
by Bernard's own disciple, Pope Eugenius III.

The vast size of the church at Cluny of which Bernard disapproved so strongly has been already mentioned. Not only was it
enormous but it was also filled with many great treasures, notably a
huge golden candelabrum. Yet this large and magnificent building
had been begun during Bernard's childhood by St. Hugh, one of
Cluny's most holy abbots. Bernard speaks of the distraction from
prayer and recollection caused by all these ornaments and treasures.
They might have distracted him but the majority of monks were
not so sensitive and would probably very soon cease to notice what
daily use had made familiar.

For the most part the monks of Cluny and other houses were
perfectly sincere in their love of the glory of God's house, but it is
clear that the attitude had its dangers. It would be all too easy for
them to forget that they were only the custodians and not the
owners of these riches. And sometimes this love of splendour in the
worship of God went too far and brought whole communities to
the verge of penury. It could also lead to other unfortunate consequences; in the year 1106 the Abbot of Vezelay levied such high
taxes in order to pay for his great church that the people rose up in
revolt and killed him.

The Cistercians, on the other hand, would have none of all this
magnificence even in the worship of God; theirs was a different but
equally legitimate ideal, and we may call it the ideal of "poverty
for God". This is the ideal of a soul who seeks and thirsts for God
alone and finds that anything apart from God is a distraction from
the "one thing necessary" of Mary who sat at the Lord's feet. It is a
superb and holy ideal but it can become false and dangerous when
it leads a man to make his own tastes into a rule for everyone. It
can lead to a specially unpleasant form of hypocrisy and intolerance.

If we would truly assess the Apologia of Bernard we must judge
it by its result on the men of his day, and there is no doubt at all
that it had a very marked effect indeed and that it has not ceased to
influence men now eight hundred years after it was published. It
was abused and misunderstood; unworthy monks in both the rival
Orders used it as ammunition in their campaign of mutual ridicule;
but far more important and far more lasting was the effect it had
on the best spirits of the time who had come to accept as inevitable
the current abuses and corruptions which Bernard pillories. For

these men it was like lightning on a dark day; in a flash their eyes were opened to their surroundings and to themselves. We have seen how Abbot Suger was converted by it, so too was Peter the Venerable. Peter had always led a holy life himself but he was spurred by the Apologia, set about correcting corruption in the houses under his jurisdiction and introducing severe reforms. And Gregory, Abbot of St. Medard, was inspired by it to summon the abbots of the diocese to his monastery at Soissons in order to discuss necessary reforms. Bernard was invited but could not come, instead he wrote a letter of encouragement. "So that those who now applaud you for what you are doing," he wrote, "may have no occasion to laugh at you and say you met for nothing, endeavour I beseech you to make good enactments, and they cannot be too good. You might perhaps be too just and even too wise, for it is written 'Be not over just' and 'Do not be more wise than it behoveth to be wise,' but it is nowhere written that you should not be too good. . . . Let them depart from me and from you who say that they do not wish to be better than their fathers. If they glory in the memory of their fathers, then let them at least imitate their sanctity while they take advantage of their dispensations and indulgences."[1]

While all this was going on, while Bernard was bestriding Christendom and laying down the law to willing and unwilling monks, Abbot Stephen Harding, the man on whom in the last resort all the responsibility fell, remained quietly in his monastery praying and working in silence,—the perfect monk who had chosen the better part.

[1] Letter 94 (Migne 91).

CHAPTER VI

HARDLY had Bernard fired off his Apologia when he was called upon to rally his own Order under a blow to its prestige and self-confidence as hard as any that he had dealt the Black Monks, only it came not from an outsider but from one of their own number. Arnold, Abbot of Morimond, the twin sister of Clairvaux, and one of the outstanding abbots in the Order, suddenly and mysteriously packed up and left his house for the Holy Land taking with him the pick of his community. These sudden disasters usually have deep roots and the roots of this disaster lay in Abbot Arnold's own character. He was a native of Cologne and, in many respects, a rather impressive personality. A hard man and very severe, but also incredibly proud and pig-headed. One of those striking men we sometimes meet who seem so strong but have, in fact, surprisingly little staying power. At first Morimond had prospered and Arnold began to have hopes of rivalling Bernard without putting himself to all the trouble of imitating his virtues. By the time of the débâcle Morimond had made as many foundations as Clairvaux. But under the surface things were not going well, the Abbot was upsetting his community by his overbearing manners, and many of his monks had begun to lose heart. On the top of this he had caused widespread scandal by an act of incredible indiscretion. He had taken away with him to Morimond the young son of the Duke of Bavaria, who had been entrusted to the Archbishop of Cologne for his education, without ever asking his parents. It was probably in order to escape from these embarrassing situations he had created for himself that he decided to leave Morimond with the pick of his monks for the Holy Land, giving out that he had obtained permission to do so from the Holy See whereas in fact he had not even consulted his Superior, the Abbot of Citeaux, or the Bishop of the diocese.

His choice of the Holy Land would have appealed to the better monks of his community. It was rapidly becoming the fashion to set off there. Several well-known people had gone, notably a relation of St. Norbert. Nevertheless, Bernard viewed with strong disfavour the fashion of monks and clergy to set out thither: "As if it were not clear to everyone," he said, "that what we want in the Holy Land is not monks to pray but soldiers to fight." One of the more human and lovable things about Bernard was that he never could quite get away from the warrior instincts he had inherited from a long line of fighting ancestors. He dearly loved a good fight if only the case was just.

Bernard was flabbergasted when the news reached him of the débâcle at Morimond. The Abbot of Citeaux was away in Flanders on business of the Order and it fell on Bernard to try to save the situation. The first thing he did was to write to Abbot Arnold, and we can at least be grateful to the unfortunate Abbot for having by his foolishness provided the occasion for one of Bernard's finest letters. "I want you to know," he wrote, "first of all that our lord of Citeaux had not returned from Flanders where he had lately gone, passing by here, when your messenger arrived. So he has not received your letter and is still ignorant of this novel venture you have undertaken. He is happy, even if only for a short time, to know nothing of the sad rumours that are going around. You have reduced me to despair by forbidding me to make any attempt to recall you and saying that it would be useless. I probably ought not to obey you in this matter and, I confess, for the very grief I feel I could not do so; although were I to know how to find you I would sooner come to you in person than write to you. . . . Confident in your own obstinacy and sure that no force, no prayers, no efforts whatsoever can turn you from your purpose, you will probably smile at what you consider my futile self-assurance. . . . Although I know something of your obstinate and stony heart, yet I wish I were by your side to persuade you even if I could achieve nothing. Whether it would be of any avail I do not know, but I would lay before you the great reasons that compel me to oppose you, I would plead with you not only by my words but also by my tears and sorrow. I would throw myself at your feet, embrace your knees, hang upon your neck and kiss your dear head, that head which has been bowed with mine in a like purpose under Christ's sweet yoke for so many years. . . . Were it only permitted me I would bend you by affection, if I could not convince you by reason! That hard heart of yours, so far proof even against the fear of Christ, I would soften with the touch of brotherly love! But alas! even this opportunity you have taken from me. Great support of our Order! Listen, I beg you, even to an absent friend wholly opposed to your venture yet sympathizing wholly with your difficulties and dangers. Great support of our Order, have you no fear at all that with your fall the collapse of the whole structure may follow?"[1] To a friend of his, Bruno of Cologne, he wrote: "Arnold, the Abbot of Morimond, has deserted his monastery unlawfully and to the great scandal of our Order. He left without waiting to consult his brother abbots or even for the permission of the Abbot of Citeaux to whom he is especially bound by obedience. He has taken with him the better and the more perfect of the great crowd of monks he collected at Morimond and left the more simple and less fervent. Amongst these there are three whose abduction especially troubles me; he has dared to lead off with him and lead astray Everard your brother, Adam whom you know well, and that noble youth Conrad whom lately, and not without scandal, he carried off from Cologne. I am fully confident that, should you endeavour to do so, you could by exerting yourself recall these men. I would not have you waste your time over Arnold, I know too well his obstinate character..."[2]

As soon as Stephen had returned and heard what had happened he summoned the abbots of the Order and ordered Bernard to write to Pope Calixtus II in their name telling him what had happened and warning him that Arnold would probably try to obtain from him permission for his wild venture. "We must inform you," Bernard wrote to the Pope, "that one of our brother abbots, styled of Morimond, has ill-advisedly left his monastery and, impelled by the spirit of frivolity, set out for Jerusalem. They say that he is going first to try whether he can in some way wring from you a licence for his blunder. If you were to countenance him at all in this matter (which God forbid) consider, we implore you, how great an occasion of harm it would be to our Order. With such an example before him any abbot would believe himself at liberty to throw over the burden of his office as soon as it became irksome, and especially would this be the case with us where the burden seems great and the honour small."[3] Unfortunately the Pope was dead before he received this letter. He died on 13th December, 1124.

There was one monk amongst the group that followed Arnold for whom Bernard felt specially responsible. He was a young monk called Adam who had come from Germany to study in the schools of France and had entered the Benedictine house at Marmoutier. Before he had been there very long he began to feel attracted by the austere ideal of the Cistercians and came to Clairvaux in order to consult Bernard. Bernard had already got himself into enough hot water by receiving at Clairvaux monks from Benedictine houses, so he sent him eventually, after he had spent a short time at Foigny, to confirm his stability at Morimond. Adam seems to have been a very fervent young man and the possibility of martyrdom at the hands of the infidel in the Holy Land appealed to him strongly, but before throwing in his lot with Abbot Arnold he visited Clairvaux to ask Bernard's advice. However no sooner had he returned to Morimond than he fell once more under the influence of Abbot Arnold and decided after all to follow him. In writing to him Bernard does not pull his punches: "Who has beguiled you, you silly young man, to break so soon the good resolutions on which you and I, with God our only witness, agreed? . . . Have you forgotten how at Marmoutier you dedicated the first fruits of your conversion; then how at Foigny you put yourself under my direction; and how at Morimond you confirmed your stability abandoning, under my advice, all idea of going on this pilgrimage or rather vagabondage with Abbot Arnold? . . . I implore you by the mercy of Christ to stay in your monastery or at least to meet me at a convenient place before you go."[1] But again Bernard was too late, Adam had already set off by the time this letter arrived.

Abbot Arnold never reached the Holy Land; he died in Flanders within a few months of leaving his monastery. When the news of Arnold's "dreadful but well deserved fate" reached Clairvaux, Bernard promptly wrote again to the monk Adam believing that if he could be persuaded to return to his monastery the others would follow him. It is a very long letter, and in it Bernard explains in detail the exact scope of monastic obedience. It is a letter worth the attention of monks and even more of their Superiors. Two extracts must suffice: "You say you have obtained permission from the Holy See. What a futile expedient! It is like the first man trying to cloak his shame with a fig leaf, as if it could be anything more than a mere cover. It would have been better had you sought the counsel rather than the permission of the Pope . . . When God said 'See to it that you do not treat these little ones with contempt,' he did not add, 'unless you have the permission of the Pope'; nor did he say,

[1] Ep. 6 (Migne 5).

'Whoever scandalizes one of these little ones without the permission of the Apostolic See . . .' It is clear that, except in the interests of truth, and there is no question of that in your case, it is never lawful for anyone to give scandal or to command what would give scandal." Then with regard to the scope of monastic obedience he says: "Not to mention anything else there are two things handed down to us who dwell in monasteries for special observance: one is submission to the abbot, the other is stability in our monastery, and these two are so to be observed that there is no conflict between them. That is to say, we should not be led by our stability to disdain subjection to the abbot, or by our subjection to the abbot to lose stability. Further if you disapprove of a monk who disobeys his abbot although he should persevere in stability, can you wonder if I blame you for making your obedience an excuse for losing your stability by leaving your monastery, especially as in our regular profession stability is explicitly promised without any mention at all of it being subject to the abbot?"[1]

It is not known exactly how this sorry affair ended but there is reason to suppose that after the death of Arnold all the others, including Adam, returned to Morimond.

[1] Ep. 8 (Migne 7).

CHAPTER VII

It was inevitable that the Cistercian reform with all its glamour of novelty and austerity should appeal strongly to the young and fervent monks in the older Benedictine houses, yet the departure of these young monks for the Cistercians did nothing at all to ease the tense situation between the two Orders. It was quite natural that the Benedictine abbots should not be best pleased to lose to a rival Order their most promising recruits. St. Benedict in his Rule forbids an abbot to receive a monk from a known monastery without his abbot's consent, but the phrase "known monastery" admits of more than one interpretation and as both the Benedictines and the Cistercians claimed St. Benedict as their father some quite lively controversy simmered and boiled over these few words. To us, at this distance of time, the sense of this phrase of St. Benedict may seem quite obvious, but it was a different matter when high feelings were clouding judgement. Thus it was possible for the abbot of a distant and remote monastery who had lost one of his best subjects to Clairvaux to argue that St. Benedict meant that no monk should be accepted from a recognized monastery without his abbot's permission. On the other hand it could be argued that St. Benedict meant a monastery that was personally known to the abbot who accepted the monk. Here were the seeds of interminable bickering. Thus a very awkward situation arose between the Abbot of St. Nicasius at Rheims, and Bernard, and Bernard's old friend Hugh of Mâcon, who had become Abbot of Pontigny, over a young monk called Drogo (what extraordinary names some of these medieval monks had!) who had left St. Nicasius in order to join Pontigny. The Abbot of St. Nicasius believed that Bernard was the nigger in the woodpile and he did certainly know something of the matter. So the angry Abbot wrote and remonstrated and Bernard answered with a tactful letter: "He who bore in his body all our griefs," he wrote, "knows how deeply I sympathize with you. I would gladly counsel you if I knew what to say, and help you if I knew what to do . . . I would certainly not have advised Brother Drogo to leave you if he had consulted me in the matter nor would I have received him here if he had come to me after leaving you! As you know I have done what I can by writing to Abbot Hugh of Pontigny who has received him."[1] Unfortunately Bernard's letter to Abbot Hugh has not survived but we know that he was not at all pleased with it and that he wrote to Bernard an indignant reply; he apparently thought Bernard wanted Drogo for Clairvaux and was annoyed at his going to Pontigny. Bernard wrote back saying: "As far as I can gather from your letter it seems that either I worded myself less clearly than I wished or else you have not understood me in the way I intended you to do. The warning I gave you of the consequences of receiving that monk from St. Nicasius was quite sincere, I really did fear them and I still do. But I had no intention at all of trying to persuade you or advise you, still less did I mean, as you seem to think I did, that he ought to be returned to his monastery. As I have known of his wish to join us for a long time I ought rather to congratulate him than persuade him to go back. But when his abbot, with whom I am very intimate, and also the Archbishop of Rheims implored me to write to you and ask for his return, I tried as far as I could to clear myself of any complicity in the affair and warn you of the ill-feeling you might stir up against yourself by accepting the monk, while at the same time satisfying them. Knowing your shrewdness I thought you would be able to read between the lines. . . ."[2]

Then he took up his pen and wrote to Drogo: "It is clear, my dear Drogo, that my affection for you has not been misplaced. Even before this happened I saw you were a very lovable person, and I believed there was something about you, I know not what, that entitled you to respect as well as affection."[3] Quite so; but after a few months at Pontigny Drogo lost heart and returned to St. Nicasius while his abbot went off to become a Carthusian.

There was also the affair of Brother Benedict, monk of St. Germer de Flay. It was the misfortune of this poor man to be skilled in the art of medicine. Hildegair, his abbot, tried to make use of his skill for the profit of the monastery. Brother Benedict protested: he had not become a monk in order to doctor secular persons. The Abbot would not listen to him, so he fled to Clairvaux. At first Bernard would not take him in and Brother Benedict went and lived in a hermitage near by. After seven months of eremitical life he applied

[1] Ep. 33 (Migne 32).
[2] Ep. 34 (Migne 33).
[3] Ep. 35 (Migne 34).

to Clairvaux again and was accepted. It must have been some time before Abbot Hildegair heard of what had happened to Brother Benedict, for it was not until after he was professed at Clairvaux that the fuss began. In reply to a very indignant letter from Hildegair remonstrating with him for having taken Brother Benedict Bernard wrote: "We understand from your letter that you are upset by our having received Brother Benedict here. We are sorry that you are sad about it because we doubt whether it is the 'sadness according to God' of which the Apostle speaks, for if it were this sort of supernatural sadness we do not think you would have reproached us so bitterly without knowing anything at all about us although we are your brothers and could be, if you wished it, your friends. . . . Taking it for granted that your monastery is well known to us you cite against us that passage of the Rule which forbids the reception of monks from a known monastery. Your monastery may be well known, but it is not so to us. . . ."[1] Unfortunately this was not to be the end of the matter, for the Abbot answered with another furious letter to which Bernard replied: "It would have been more becoming if you had been content with my last reply to your complaints and ceased from your uncalled-for invectives. But as to your former charges you have now added worse ones and tried once more to give me grounds for quarrelling, I shall truthfully answer a second time the accusations you impudently cast at my head, lest if I say nothing at all my silence should be taken as an admission of guilt. . . . As far as I can make out the great injury I have done you, my whole fault amounts to nothing more than this, that I have opened the doors of my monastery to a lonely, strange, poor and unhappy monk who, fleeing from danger to his soul and seeking salvation, knocked at our door and implored to be admitted; and that I refuse to turn out again without sufficient reasons the man I have received in these circumstances. . . . The only ground for inquiry between us, the only thing that remains to be discovered, is whether I did right to receive him. And you, for your part, as you cannot deny that a monk may be lawfully received from an unknown monastery, contend that you are not unknown to me. I deny this, I deny that I know anything of you, but you will not believe me. . . . Cease therefore, my brothers, cease worrying your brother whom you have no cause to worry, unless perhaps it is your own interests and not God's glory you are seeking, your own satis-

[1] Ep. 70 (Migne 67).

faction in your brother's return and not the salvation of his soul. Since you say he was always a rolling stone with you and, contrary to his state and the commands of his abbot, spent the money he made in the practice of his art upon himself, if you love him you should be glad that he is now cured. I assure you that he never wanders abroad now but peacefully in the monastery he lives without complaint amongst poor men the life of a poor man."[1]

But we must not believe that Bernard deliberately fished for recruits in other people's waters. He seems never to have invited monks to Clairvaux from other houses, nor did he always accept them when they came. There is evidence in plenty to indicate that he acted with the utmost good sense and discretion in this matter, at any rate after he had burned his fingers once or twice. Unless there were very good reasons for receiving a fugitive monk or unless he believed he could accept him without stirring up trouble, he sent him back to his monastery with a covering letter to his abbot. Thus he writes to one abbot: "I am returning Brother Lambert to you. I have carefully inquired into the cause of his coming here and also his reasons for leaving you. His intentions seem to have been above reproach, but he certainly had no excuse for leaving you in the way he did."[2] And to Abbot Simon of St. Nicolas he writes: "You see it was for very good reasons that I have acted contrary to my usual practice by keeping your stray sheep here for a time. I did not do it for my own sake, but for both yours and his, so that I might be able to kill two birds with one stone by satisfying both his desire for a stricter life and yours that he should stay at home. . . . A monk who is unsettled and dissatisfied may often be quickly reconciled to the life in his own monastery by the experience of something a little more strict."[3] Here speaks an abbot of mature experience and, perhaps, the disillusionment that comes from experience. We are all perhaps a little too prone to think that Saints are born holy, wise, and discreet. This is never the case, they are born like all of us with the stain of original sin and all its consequences; it takes time for them to mature in sanctity and to profit from their experience.

Although ill-feeling and controversy were constantly flaming up here and there between the Cistercians and the older Orders, there

[1] Ep. 71 (Migne 68).
[2] Ep. 102 (Migne 101).
[3] Ep. 86 (Migne 84).

can be no doubt that many abbots and monks were big enough men to learn from the example of the Cistercian reform how to put their own houses in order. Sometimes Bernard was even obliged to restrain the reforming zeal of abbots and counsel moderation. Thus to an abbot of a Benedictine house he wrote: "I could not but feel for you when I read in your letter of the persecutions you are obliged to endure for the sake of justice. . . . I counsel you, Reverend Father, to moderate the full vigour of your purpose and of those who side with you so as not to ignore the welfare of weaker souls. The monks of the Cluniac observance over whom you rule should be invited but not forced to a stricter way of life."[1]

Bernard's influence and fame was not limited to the Continent, it penetrated even into the mists and rain of England. In the year 1132 it had filtered into the cloisters of St. Mary's Abbey, York, causing some of the young monks there to dream dreams of reform and trouble the rather comatose life of their brethren. The Abbey had become rich and, if one may believe the evidence of the Archbishop of York, had adopted rather more than all the usual mitigations of St. Benedict's Rule. But there was an élite led by Richard the prior and Gervase the sub-Prior who were not satisfied with this half-hearted observance, and they drew up a scheme of reform and presented it to their abbot. Abbot Geoffrey was a man of peace; he had reached the time of life when a man begins to hope that having got so far without trouble he may be able to spend the days that remain to him in peace; he was also an illiterate and rather muddle-headed old gentleman. As we should expect of such a man, he tried to put off the reformers by saying that it would be very difficult to change long-established customs, and he suggested that they should go away and let the matter rest until the feast of the Nativity of Our Lady, when he would tell them what he had decided. By this time news of the proposed reforms had spread amongst the brethren and stormy scenes ensued. Richard and his followers went to Thurston the Archbishop of York and opened their hearts to him. He encouraged them in their scheme and summoned them to his palace with their abbot to discuss the matter. At the meeting Richard said that all he and his followers wanted was to be allowed to follow Christ in poverty according to the Holy Rule. Abbot Geoffrey wept and promised that he would not do anything to prevent them. Then the Archbishop suggested that

[1] Ep. 85 (Migne 83).

he should meet the community in Chapter and see what could be arranged. He arrived at the Abbey accompanied by certain discreet and learned members of his household to find, instead of the respectful welcome he had expected, Abbot Geoffrey surrounded by a crowd of infuriated monks barring the way to the Chapter-house. The Archbishop, rather embarrassed by this sudden change in the situation, tried to remonstrate but could not make his voice heard above the din of shouting and bawling monks. He tried to point out that he had only come as their friend and father in God. But the monks would not listen to him and set about trying to throw him out. The reformers, scared out of their wits at the tumult, clung to the Archbishop for protection and together they tried to fight their way out with such dignity as they could muster. "Hold them! Hold them!" cried the monks, but they managed to slip through their clutches and escape with nothing worse than a few bruises. As the Archbishop rode away he shouted out that he had put the house under an interdict, "better a century of interdict," rejoined the monks, "than the interference of an Archbishop."[1]

There were altogether about thirteen reformers and they remained with the Archbishop for three months, during which time two of them thought better of their action and returned to St. Mary's Abbey; these were Gervase the sub-Prior and a monk called Ralph. The remainder were installed on Christmas Day of the same year by the Archbishop on his own land at Skeldale, a wild and uncultivated wilderness, and Richard became their abbot. In the meantime Abbot Geoffrey, who must have been a rather naïve old man, wrote to Bernard apparently to try and enlist him on his side. Bernard replied with what was, for him, a rather careful letter, but he left no doubt as to where his sympathies lay.

Things did not go easily at Skeldale. Richard and his companions were reduced to complete penury, but they persevered and eventually wrote to Bernard for help. Bernard replied in his most enthusiastic manner and promised to send Brother Geoffrey to help them. This was Geoffrey of Ainai, an experienced and elderly monk. Their affiliation to Clairvaux followed in the year 1134. Thus from these pangs was born the great Abbey of Fountains to be for long years a source of spiritual light in the North of England until at last

[1] The letter of Archbishop Thurston to William Archbishop of Canterbury, in the collection of St. Bernard's Letters in Migne 490. A lively and presumably accurate account of the incident.

it lost touch with its source of life and withered away in the storm of the Reformation. As the riches and buildings of the monks grew so did their fervour and numbers decline, until there was no strength left to withstand the storm when it broke. The beginnings of this great Abbey were painful, its youth was grand, and in old age it met with the fate that awaits all human achievement.

Bernard's relations with the Carthusian hermits were consistently cordial and there was nothing he loved more than to visit the Grande Chartreuse, the mother-house of the Order far away up in the mountains of Savoy where it remains alive and flourishing to this day. An anecdote is told of one of his visits there that bears the impress of truth. The good hermits were most edified and charmed by their distinguished guest, but there was one thing that a little surprised and even shocked them. Bernard, the great protagonist of holy poverty, had arrived on a superb and gaily caparisoned horse! At last one of them summoned up courage to ask Bernard how he came by such a grand equipage. But no one could have been more amazed than Bernard when it was pointed out to him! He had borrowed the animal and its harness without bothering to look at it. So the anecdote ends, as all anecdotes of Saints are supposed to end, in general edification. Whether true or not, it well illustrates Bernard's gift of being able to lay aside all his cares at the first opportunity and become completely absorbed in prayer. Even when all Europe was waiting on his word and messengers were arriving almost every hour at Clairvaux, at the first moment of respite his spirit turned to God as surely as steel to a magnet. No one with any acquaintance at all with his writings can doubt that he remained all his life first and foremost a monk.

Bernard's contacts with the Carthusians remained throughout his life so close that it has even been said, although without any evidence, that he tried his vocation with them. There is no doubt at all that he would have wished to do so in order to escape from his cares, but the life was not for him. It was to the Prior of the Grande Chartreuse that he addressed his well-known and deservedly famous letter on the love of God.

Here in this letter we find the real Bernard, not the whole of him but the heart of him. The world might admire and rightly admire his immense courage, his massive personality, his wonderful eloquence, and the flash of his humour, but the thing that united all these natural gifts into one flaming brand was his white-hot charity;

it transmuted the whole of his personality into the torch that set the hearts of men on fire. "I congratulate you," he writes to the Prior, "on your charity, and myself on the profit that my soul has derived from it. For that is true and sincere charity to be attributed entirely to a pure heart and unfeigned faith which leads us to love our neighbours' good as well as our own. The man who loves his own good in preference to his neighbours' good or who loves only his own good proves, by the very fact that his love is not disinterested, that he does not love the good with a chaste love. Such a one could not obey the Prophet when he says: 'Praise the Lord because he is good.' He may praise the Lord because he is good to himself, but not because he is Goodness itself. . . . There are those who praise the Lord because he is powerful, and these are slaves and fearful for themselves; there are those who praise him because he is good to them, and these are hirelings seeking themselves; and there are those who praise him because he is Goodness itself, and these are sons doing homage to their father. But those who fear for themselves and those who seek themselves are acting only for themselves; only the love of a son seeks not itself. On this account I think that the words 'The Law of God is unspotted' refer to charity, because it alone can turn the heart from love of self and the world, and direct it to God alone. . . .

"I would call his charity unspotted who never keeps anything of his own for himself. When a man keeps nothing of his own for himself, everything he has is God's, and what is God's cannot be unclean. Therefore the unspotted law of God is charity, which seeks not what may benefit itself, but what may benefit many. Charity is called the law of the Lord, either because the Lord himself lives by it or else because none may have it save by his gift. Let it not seem absurd that I should have said that even God lives by law, for I have also said that the law is nothing else but charity. What else but charity preserves that supreme and unspeakable unity in the blessed Trinity? Charity is therefore a law, and it is the law of the Lord holding together, as it were, the Trinity and binding it in the bonds of peace. Yet let no one think that I speak of charity here as if it were a quality or something accidental to the Godhead, as if I were saying (may it be far from me to say any such thing!) that there was something in God which is not God; but I say that charity is the divine substance itself. And there is nothing new or strange about this, for St. John himself has said, 'God is charity.' It follows that charity can be correctly said to be both God and the gift of God; that charity gives charity; the substance of charity, the quality of charity. When we speak of the giver we mean the substance; when we speak of the gift we mean the quality. This is eternal law, the creator and ruler of the universe, since through it all things were made in weight, measure, and number. Nothing is left without law, since even the law of all things is not without a law, yet a law not other than itself for, although it did not create itself, it nevertheless rules itself.

"The slave and hireling also have a law, a law not from God, but which they make for themselves; the one by not loving God and the other by loving something besides God. . . . Anyone can make a law for himself, but he cannot withdraw it from the immutable order of the eternal law. But anyone who makes a law for himself is perversely trying to imitate his Creator by ruling himself and making his own self-will a law for himself, just as God is his own law and subject only to himself. Alas! what a heavy and unsupportable burden is this on the children of Adam; we are bowed down and bent under it, so that our lives are dragged down to the very brink of hell. It is the property of the eternal law of God that he who will not be ruled sweetly by him, shall be ruled as a punishment by himself; that he who, of his own will, throws off the sweet and light yoke of charity shall unwillingly suffer the insupportable burden of his own self-will.

"Good and sweet is the law of charity, not only light to bear, but also an easement of the law of slaves and hirelings. For it does not destroy these laws, it brings them to perfection, according to our Lord's words: 'I have not come to set aside the law, but to bring it to perfection.' Tempering the one and controlling the other, it eases both. Charity will never be without fear, but a chaste fear; nor ever without self-interest, but an ordered self-interest. When devotion is mixed with fear it does not nullify it, but amends it; it takes from it the anguish which it never lacks when it is servile, and renders it chaste and filial. . . . And the self-interest inherent in the law of the hireling is controlled by charity, so that it entirely rejects what is evil, prefers what is better to what is good, and what is good only for the sake of what is better. And, when this is fully effected in the soul by the grace of God, the body and all created good are only loved for the sake of the soul, and the soul only for the sake of God, and God for his own sake.

"Because we are flesh and blood born of the desire of the flesh, our desire or love must start in the flesh, and it will then, if properly directed, progress under grace by certain stages until it is fulfilled in the spirit, for 'that was not first which is spiritual, but that which is natural; afterwards that which is spiritual', and we must first bear the image which is earthly and afterwards that which is heavenly. At first a man loves himself for his own sake. He is flesh and is able only to know himself. But when he sees that he cannot subsist of himself, then he begins by faith to seek and love God as necessary to himself. And so in the second stage he loves God, not yet for God's sake, but for his own sake. However when, on account of his own necessity, he begins to meditate, read, pray, and obey, he becomes accustomed little by little to know God and consequently to delight in him. When he has tasted and found how sweet is the Lord he passes to the third stage wherein he loves God for God's sake and not for his own. And here he remains, for I doubt whether the fourth stage has ever been reached in this life by any man, the stage, that is, wherein a man loves himself only for God's sake. Let those say who have experienced it; I confess that to me it seems impossible. It will come about, doubtless, when the good and faithful servant shall have been brought into the joy of the Lord and become inebriated with the fulness of the house of God. For he will then be wholly lost in God as one inebriated and henceforth cleave to him as if one in spirit with him, forgetful, in a wonderful manner, of himself and, as it were, completely out of himself."

Hardly less cordial were Bernard's relations with the Premonstratensian Canons. He was on intimate and most friendly terms with the founder, St. Norbert, and he seems to have helped him to obtain the land for his first foundation at Premontré by generously relinquishing the prior claim that he had on it for one of his own foundations. An agreement was signed between the two Orders that they would not receive men from each other's houses, and the influence of the Cistercians on the Premonstratensians was so great that for austerity of life there was at first little to choose between them.

About the year 1119 a certain Hugh de Payne, with six other knights, formed a group bound together by the three canonical vows, for the purpose of protecting pilgrims to the Holy Land. We know little more about the origin of these Knights of the

Temple, as they were called, until Hugh sought the approval of the Church for his venture at the Council of Troyes in the year 1128. Bernard was present at this Council and so also were Stephen Harding and several other Cistercian abbots. The Rule for the Knights was presented to the assembled fathers and, most probably under Bernard's influence, it was formally accepted. It has been thought that Bernard had a hand in framing the Rule and it is most probable that he did have, for the whole ideal of the Knights was very much in accordance with his own temper, and the quasi-monastic spirit of the Order is unmistakable. A little later Hugh asked Bernard to write an apologia for the new Knighthood and he enthusiastically agreed to do so, calling the treatise "In Praise of the New Knighthood". The theme is very different from that of his letter to the Carthusians on the Love of God or any of his other treatises and sermons, yet the charity and fervent sincerity behind it is the same and unmistakably Bernard's. Very appropriately he starts off with a rousing trumpet-call: "The news has gone forth that a new Knighthood has arisen on earth, and on that part of the earth where the Day Star dwelt amongst us clothed in flesh and blood. In the land where he overthrew the princes of darkness in the strength of his own right hand, there too he will now wipe out the unbelievers their satellites by the strength of these mighty warriors saving his people and once again lifting up the horn of his salvation in the house of David his son."[1] After this fine beginning he goes on to describe the life of these new Knights: "For the confusion of our own knights, knights more of the devil than of God, let me briefly describe the life and conduct of these Knights of Christ. . . . First of all they live under discipline. Their going out and their coming in is at the command of their Superior. They wear what they are given and do not presume to seek their food or their apparel elsewhere. In both food and clothes only necessity is considered. They live a joyous but frugal life in common without wives and without children. And so that nothing may be lacking to their state of evangelical perfection they all live the same life without anyone of them having property of his own, maintaining unity in the bonds of peace. There is no accepting of persons amongst them. The better man and not the better born is put first. Lions in battle, they are lambs at home. They do not consider the numbers or advantages of their adversary but, confident in the help of the Most

[1] Ad Milites Templi de laude novae Militiae liber.

High, where the fighting is hottest there they will be found. Gentle to orphans and widows, they are terrible to the proud and truculent. God has chosen these men from the strong men of the most distant parts of the earth, to serve him and to guard the most holy sepulchre of Christ. Both monks and knights, they lack neither the gentleness and austerity of the former nor the spirit and courage of the latter."[1]

Perhaps it is asking too much of human nature to expect men to live for long the life of a soldier according to these high ideals. Yet the Knights of the Temple, however sad and perhaps sordid their end, fulfilled a noble purpose in their day. The mere presence of knights trying sincerely to be knights of Christ and, above all, independent of the feudal lords, did very much to raise the whole tone of warfare and to check the worst excesses of the common soldiery.

Bernard's relations with nuns were various and frequent but, for the most part, he seems to have kept himself aloof from individual contacts and to have concerned himself mainly with trying to reform convents that stood in need of it. There is one letter of his to St. Hildegarde. Hildegarde was a visionary favoured with many rather surprising revelations that were more generally admired than widely understood. She had written to Bernard to tell him that she had seen him in a vision as "a man in the sun". Bernard wrote back: "That other people should believe me to be better than I know myself to be, is an indication more of human stupidity than of any virtues in myself. . . . I congratulate you on the grace of God that is in you and admonish you to regard it as a gift and to respond to it with humility and devotion." As Hildegarde was a Saint it is to be supposed that she took this letter in good part. To a nun who had suddenly conceived the desire to live as an anchorite he wrote: ". . . before the reform of your convent you never, so far as I know, mentioned this plan of yours to anyone. But only when Religion began to flourish in your house did you suddenly become holy and, fired by unexpected fervour, begin to think of the desert."[2] Bernard was an idealist and a great mystic, but he was also a realist with a shrewd understanding of human nature. His heart may have been in heaven, as it undoubtedly was, but he kept his feet on the ground and, most of the time, he looked where he was going.

It is sometimes said that Bernard did not, in his heart of hearts,

[1] Ibid.
[2] Ep. 390 (Migne 366). Ep. 118 (Migne 115).

believe that there was any salvation outside Clairvaux, and it must be confessed that he sometimes gives that impression. It is true that he does not seem to have had the modern idea of the monastic vocation, that it is a way of life only possible and only desirable for a small and select body of men. His true and considered opinion seems to have been that the monastic way of life was the safest and that the way of life at Clairvaux was the safest of all. He seemed to believe that although the monastic life was clearly impossible for most men as a consequence of their circumstances and the frailty of human nature, yet antecedently it was desirable for all and the only way of salvation for some. Passions ran higher in those days, men were less inhibited then than now. The strong conventions of a society nearly eight hundred years older than Bernard's are, or were until lately, some sort of a curb on the more boisterous passions. Society in Bernard's day was still in its youth with all the soaring ideals and surging passions of youth. There can be little doubt that there were men in those days who needed the strong discipline of the monastic régime if they were to save their souls. For men like this it must be all or nothing, and it is perhaps our loss that there are fewer men of this calibre today and that they usually find their way into the camp of the adversary. For men like this Bernard believed that without any doubt the life at Clairvaux was the best and the safest if not quite the only way to salvation. He did not stop to consider, as we should, if they had a vocation, he did not look at it in that way at all. He would probably have said that if a man does his best, grace will come to his aid and that he would be there to see that the man did do his best. It is clear that Bernard himself was like this. An ordinary good life in the world would have been impossible for a man of his ardent and impetuous emotions. By nature he was prone to extremes. Of such material Saints are made, but Saints of Bernard's pattern, Sons of Thunder, not the careful child Saints of our times; in Bernard's day suburbia had not been born. There is a story told of how he rescued a murderer from the gallows and led him off in triumph to Clairvaux there to expiate his crimes not on the gallows but on the cross. Perhaps a modern abbot would have hesitated before doing this to ask himself if the man had a true vocation. But Bernard does not appear to have been in two minds on the matter, it was obvious to him that it would be better for the man to spend his life at Clairvaux and perhaps die a Saint, and he was right, the man did die a Saint. Is it possible that the singular dearth

of at any rate canonized Saints in our modern monasteries is due to
their inability to "digest" men like this? Would even Bernard have
been accepted in our monasteries?

But there were others besides men of this sort who Bernard
believed should be monks of Clairvaux, young men of noble birth
and refined scholarly tastes. "I am filled with sorrow," he wrote to
one young man, "when I think of the flower of your youth, the
brightness of your intelligence, the ornaments of your scholarship
and, what better becomes a Christian, your noble bearing, all being
wasted in futile pursuits when they could be so much better employed in the service of Christ".[1] There are many letters like this
from Bernard to the *jeunesse dorée* of his day. And there is one superb
passage in a letter he wrote to Alexander the Bishop of Lincoln,
surnamed the Magnificent, to break the news to him that one of his
favourite clerics, who had gone on pilgrimage to the Holy Land,
had entered Clairvaux. It is important not only for its beauty and
eloquence but for the clear idea it gives of how Bernard regarded
the life at Clairvaux: "I write to tell you," he says, "that your Philip
has found a short cut to Jerusalem and has arrived there very quickly.
He crossed 'the vast ocean stretching wide on every hand' with a
favourable wind in a very short time, and he has now cast anchor
on the shores for which he was making. Even now he stands in the
courts of Jerusalem and 'whom he heard tidings of in Ephrata he
has found in the woodland plains' and gladly reverences in the place
where he has halted his journey. He has entered the Holy City and
has chosen his heritage with them of whom it has been said: 'You
are no longer aliens; the saints are your fellow-citizens, you belong
to God's household.' His going and coming is in their company
and he has become one of them, glorifying God and saying with
them, 'We find our true home in heaven.' He is no longer an
inquisitive onlooker, but a devout inhabitant and an enrolled citizen
of Jerusalem; not of that earthly Jerusalem to which Mount Sinai in
Arabia is joined, and which is in bondage with her children, but of
that free Jerusalem which is above and the mother of us all. And
this, if you want to know, is Clairvaux. She is the Jerusalem united
to the one in heaven by whole-hearted devotion, by conformity of
life, and by a certain spiritual affinity."[2] Was there ever a more
compelling description of the monastic life? Surely there is no one

[1] Ep. 105 (Migne 104).
[2] Ep. 67 (Migne 64).

who can read it without a bitter regret that the fair flower of Clairvaux withered so soon leaving only the empty and outrageous husk.
The fine letter he wrote to encourage parents who had lost their only
son to Clairvaux assuring them that they need not worry about his
health because he would so arrange things for him that his body did
not suffer while his soul prospered has already been quoted;[1] it
shows very well how far Bernard was in his mature years from the
grim and intolerant abbot who considered only details of observance
as essential. But Bernard was not only concerned with the welfare of
potential recruits to Clairvaux; there is one letter of his to the mother
of a rather wild young man showing how understanding and tolerant he could be of the follies of youth. "I am sorry to hear your
son has behaved badly towards you," he wrote to the anxious
mother, "I deplore as much the conduct of the son as the wrongs of
the mother. But youth is ever prone to these follies; 'tis the hot
condition of their blood, and they are surely excusable in a young
man. . . . He has many excellent qualities and we must pray that
God may enable him in time (as I am sure he will) to emulate the
virtues of his father. Treat him gently and with forbearance,
because you are more likely to encourage him to mend his ways like
this than if you exasperated him with constant nagging. I could wish
that his conduct towards others were as irreproachable as it always is
towards myself. May God reward him for this."[2]

We have already seen how for Bernard the monastic life was no
garden enclosed reserved for a few chosen souls, but more a net
let down into the sea and landing on the shores of eternity every sort
of fish, and we have already seen how all over Europe young men
and old, noble and obscure, heard his call to leave all, and naked to
follow the naked Christ, until at last it seemed as if all the world
were becoming Cistercian. It could be argued quite plausibly that
in this Bernard defeated his own object; that in over-forcing the
monastic growth, he prepared the way for a reaction; that when his
guiding hand, his inspiring leadership was removed there was no
one else to take his place and hold up to their high purpose the discordant elements he had introduced. Certain it is that with his
death the vision faded; for a time the observance was maintained,
but with Bernard and his immediate contemporaries and disciples
the life went out of the body and it took on the rigidity of a corpse.

[1] Ep. 112 (Migne 110), quoted above Ch. III.
[2] Ep. 365 (Migne 300).

Presently even this disintegrated. Riches and prosperity ate into the heart of the Order. Abbots became great administrators rather than great men of prayer, and soon they adopted all the frills of prelacy which Bernard and the first fathers of the Order had repudiated as unbecoming in a monk. Reformers came along in their time, but though they might restore again the old observance they could not bring back the mystical and contemplative spirit which give liberty as well as life. They restored the body but they could not bring back the soul.

CHAPTER VIII

JUDGING by ordinary standards Bernard could not have been a good abbot: he was away from his monastery far too much; it has been estimated that his absences from Clairvaux amounted to a third of the time he was abbot and this does not include the long periods when he was ill.[1] Even while at Clairvaux he could not have had much time for his monks as messengers and visitors would have been coming and going all day and his correspondence must have been, for those days, enormous; enough to keep at least two secretaries busy. Yet in spite of all this by the year 1130 he had no less than two hundred monks under him. His letters are full of references to his incessant worries and occupations, of which the following is typical: ". . . because of the short summer nights and the full days I have not had one moment of leisure in which to attend to your business. Your letter found me so occupied that even to recount all I have to do would take too long, I scarcely had time to read it when it came during my dinner. By getting up early I am just able to scribble on the quiet this brief reply."[2] There is a rather touching allusion to the same thing in his fifty-second sermon of the Song of Songs: "I wish some of you sitting there would think of the respect you owe to your Superiors and bear in mind that by needlessly bothering them you make yourselves tiresome even to the citizens of heaven. You know how seldom I have an hour free from the demands of visitors. But I mention this with diffidence lest some timorous brethren might hide their troubles beyond their capacity to endure them for fear of disturbing me."[3] Yet for all his prolonged absences and incessant occupation with affairs outside his monastery, there seems to be no doubt that the whole life at Clairvaux centred in him. By ordinary standards he may not have been a good abbot, but he cannot be judged by ordinary standards. He seems to have had a wonderful gift of knowing how any of his monks felt and even while he was away his presence seemed to pervade the whole monastery. And when he was amongst his monks how much he had to give them! It was the custom of Cistercian abbots to preach in

[1] R. Fossier, op. cit., p. 97.
[2] Ep. 91 (Migne 88).
[3] Serm. in Cant. 52.7.

Chapter to their monks, but Bernard's were very different from the common run of Chapter sermons; even in the dry pages of Migne at this distance of time his vibrating personality seems to reach out to us. They give the impression of being completely spontaneous, but we know from what he tells us how carefully he prepared them, how long he prayed over them. He did not settle down with paper and pen to make notes; that was not his method; he would take the text on which he was to preach and meditate on it and pray over it. In a vivid phrase he likens the text to heavenly bread that must be cooked by meditation and prayer before it is ready to give out to others. Outstanding amongst all his sermons are those he preached on the Song of Songs. It seems doubtful whether he actually preached them to his monks, at any rate in the form that we have them, yet they are priceless not only for their doctrine and eloquence but also for the way Bernard reveals himself in them. Sometimes he even does this directly: "I admit," he says in one sermon, "that even me the Word has visited and, I speak as a fool, not infrequently. Often when he has come to me, I have not known his coming. I have been aware of his presence, I remember him to have been present, and sometimes I have even been able to tell when he would come, but never the moment of his coming nor yet of his departure."[1] And sometimes he lifts the curtain and enables us to peer round and see something of how things happened from day to day at Clairvaux. Certainly not even at Clairvaux were all the monks saints, and no one was better aware of this than Bernard. Thus commenting on the text from the Book of Wisdom: "I have treasured wisdom more than health and beauty," he says. "If more than health and beauty, how much more than pleasures and shamefulness? What does it profit a monk to restrain himself from pleasures if he is always bothering about the appearance of his food and how it is served? Vegetables, he says, give me wind, cheese weighs down my stomach, milk is bad for my head, my chest suffers if I drink water, beans make me melancholy, leeks heat my blood, fish from ponds and muddy water spoil my complexion. O I beg you have pity on your own peace of mind and on those who wait on you; try not to burden the house and consider a little the good of your soul,"[2] and then again in another sermon: "The long Vigils last night excuse your yawns, but what am I to say to those

---

[1] Serm. in Cant. 74.5.
[2] Serm. in Cant. 30.11.

who slept at the Vigils and are sleeping now?"[1] He seems to have
found it rather hard to endure fools with composure and he describes
with devastating humility how on one occasion he lost his temper
with a monk: "One day I commanded, with angry voice and threatening looks, my brother who had upset me to leave the monastery.
He immediately betook himself to one of the granges and remained
there. When I found out where he was I wanted to recall him, but
he said he would not come back unless he was first reinstated in his
old position, and not put in the last place as if he had been a runaway;
for he had been turned out of the monastery, so he said, without
consideration and without his case being heard, and that as he had
not been given a fair trial when he was turned out, he ought not to
be made to submit to judgement when he came back. As I could
not trust my own judgement in the matter owing to my natural
feelings about it, I submitted it to the consideration of the brethren.
And they, when I was absent, ruled that the brother should not be
subjected to the discipline of the rule on being received back as his
expulsion had not been according to the rule."[2]

Bernard was shrewd in his judgements of others but he was not
infallible; like all of us he could be deceived. There is the well-
known case of his secretary Nicolas. This Nicolas had been a monk
of Montier-Ramay near Troyes and impelled by a probably quite
sincere desire for a more austere life he had applied for admission to
Clairvaux and had been accepted; rather suspiciously his abbot does
not seem to have made any difficulty about his leaving. He seems
to have been very intelligent, and it was not long before Bernard
had appointed him his secretary, and he appears to have been completely hoodwinked by him. Apparently he accompanied Bernard
on some of his visits and missions and in the course of these in-
gratiated himself with Peter the Venerable. We constantly find
affectionate references to him in Bernard's letters to Peter such as
"my Nicolas, who is also yours, sends his love" and sometimes
Nicolas himself would add a postscript of affectionate greetings. At
least once Peter asked Bernard to lend him Nicolas to cheer him up
and help him. Then a rather sinister note appears in Bernard's
letters: "I am in danger from false brethren. Many forged letters

[1] Serm. in Cant. 36.7.
[2] Ep. 73 (Migne 70).

There is no doubt that this extract is genuine although it was suppressed in all the
Manuscripts at Clairvaux, v. Dom Jean Leclercq. Etudes sur. S. Bernard. Analecta
Sacri Ord. Cist., p. 91.

have gone out under my seal . . . therefore, as you will see, I have discarded my old seal and adopted a new one bearing both my image and name."[1] There soon follows a letter of wonderful invective: "A serpent has deceived me! A double-faced cunning wretch, completely devoid of any righteousness, an enemy to his own soul. . . ."[2] Finally he writes: "Nicolas has left us because he was not of us. But he has gone leaving foul traces behind him. I knew for some time what sort of man he was, but I was waiting either for God to convert him or for him to betray himself like Judas and this is what has happened. When he left us there was found on his person, besides books, money, and much gold, three seals one of which was mine, one his own, and the other the Prior's. . . . It has been partly proved and he has admitted that he has written to you falsely in my name not once but several times. His foul deeds have poisoned the very ground and are a byword with everyone, but I will not pollute my lips or your ears by mentioning them. . . . No one has better deserved a sentence of life imprisonment."[3] So that is the end of Nicolas. Evidently Bernard felt very sore about him and with good reason. But Nicolas does not seem entirely to blame for it is clear that he had been spoiled and his head turned by the attentions of Bernard and Peter. It is difficult not to believe that these two distinguished men had been rather foolish about the young man.

St. Gregory tells us that if we would know what sort of man St. Benedict was we must read the description in his Rule of what sort of man the Abbot should be. The same is true of Bernard; if we would know what sort of abbot he was, we must see what he expected of the abbots under him in the daughter houses of Clairvaux. There is one very revealing letter which he wrote to a certain Rainald, a very favourite son of his, who had become abbot of Foigny in 1121. We have already mentioned this letter but it will bear quoting more fully for the picture it gives of Bernard himself. "When you wring your hands over your many troubles, dearest Rainald, I too am moved to tears." This is how he begins, and then he goes on to say, "You must understand that you are especially the abbot of the sad, faint-hearted, and discontented amongst your flock. It is by consoling, encouraging, and admonishing them that

[1] Ep. 354 (Migne 284).
[2] Ep. 339 (Migne 269).
[3] Ep. 363 (Migne 298).

you do your duty and carry your burden and, by carrying your burden, heal those whom you carry. If there is anyone so spiritually strong that he rather helps you than is helped by you, you are not so much his father as his equal, not so much his abbot as his fellow. Why then complain that you find the company of some of those over whom you rule more of a burden than a comfort? You were given to them as their abbot not to be comforted but to comfort because you were the strongest of them all. . . . You should understand that you are sent not to be helped but to help, and that you hold the place of him who came not to be served but to serve."[1] It is a great temptation to go on quoting from these charming and human letters Bernard wrote to the monks he had sent out as abbots of new foundations. To the same Rainald he writes again disclaiming the high titles he had given him and quoting a tag from Ovid, "your favourite Ovid", to comfort him. Monks reading Ovid!—one wonders what some of the old Trappists would have thought of that! He ends one letter to Baldwin, Abbot of Rieti, saying: "Alas! I am called away. I have no time to write more. Let me urge you to free me of one heavy care by telling me what you meant when you said that someone whom you would never have expected had wounded you. This gives me much anxiety."[2] Finally there is the letter he wrote to an unknown abbot who was worried about a disobedient monk; it is a fine commentary on the twenty-eighth chapter of St. Benedict's Rule: "About that troubled and troublesome brother," he writes. "It is the endeavour of the devil to go around the house of God seeking whom he may devour, and it is your duty to keep a sharp lookout so that he may not find a way in. The more he tries to separate a weak lamb from the rest of the flock the more you must withstand him with all your might. Do all that charity requires to save the brother; spare neither kindness, wholesome advice, rebukes in private, exhortations in public, nor, if necessary, sharp words and sharp floggings; but above all do not spare what is usually more efficacious than anything else in these cases, and that is your prayers and the prayers of the brethren. If you have done all this and it has availed nothing, then you must have recourse to the advice of the Apostle and 'put away the evil one', lest he lead others into evil."[3]

[1] Ep. 76 (Migne 73).
[2] Ep. 259 (Migne 201).
[3] Ep. 103 (Migne 102).

This then is Bernard amongst his monks: very busy, preoccupied, and tired, apt to be impatient and to flare up; but infinitely kind, tolerant, and human. Certainly a man of God and a man of prayer, but with nothing of the vague visionary about him. He had a genius for inspiring affection and trust amongst his subjects as well as amongst his equals. There must have been something quite unique about Clairvaux in his day. Hardly could he persuade his monks to leave it in order to be abbots of other monasteries or to make foundations in other parts of Europe, and hardly had they gone before they were sighing to come back. Constantly Bernard had to write and assure them that although they were far away they would return to Clairvaux to die.

CHAPTER IX

IT is universally recognized that Bernard was not only a monk but also a great mystic, but it is sometimes forgotten that he was besides this what one can only call a man of the Church, that is to say he felt all the trials and sufferings of the Church as if they were his own, indeed a great deal more acutely than he felt his own. Viewing from the cloister the luxury of the clergy and all the abuses prevalent in the Church he did not feel they were no concern of his, but with St. Paul he felt constrained to cry: "Is anyone's conscience hurt? I am aflame." Yet he did not believe it was therefore his business to interfere; only in deference to the commands of the bishop of his diocese or some higher authority could he be persuaded to leave his monastery.

It may seem incongruous to us that a monk of what we should call a "Contemplation Order" should have immersed himself so completely as Bernard seems to have done in affairs that concerned him but little. Yet we must remember that he only did so under the compulsion of obedience and we must bear in mind that he would not have understood our hard and fast distinction between the contemplative life and the active life; for him the distinction lay between contemplation and action. He would have said that at Clairvaux some of his monks were leading the contemplative life with Mary and others the active life with Martha, and by the active life he would have meant almost precisely what we mean by the Purgative Way. As for contemplation and action, he held that while contemplation was more perfect and better than action in that it was a foretaste of the next life, action was sometimes of greater moment than contemplation and should, on occasion, be preferred to it. He believed it was wrong for anyone to ignore his neighbour's needs and necessities for the sake of contemplation if he had the power to relieve them or if he was bound by his state of life to try to relieve them. Thus to his friend Canon Oger, who had given up the cure of souls for the sake of what we should call a life of prayer, he wrote: "I gather from your letter that you have found your pastoral charge irksome and have relinquished it after having not so much asked your bishop's permission as exacted it by your insistence. I very much fear that in thus disburdening yourself you have dishonoured God. . . . Better tell the truth and admit that your own quiet pleased you more than labouring for the benefit of others. Either you should not have undertaken the cure of souls or, having once undertaken it, you should on no account have relinquished it."[1] And to the Archbishop of York, who desired to leave his See and become a monk, he wrote: "I praise your desire for quiet and your wish to rest peacefully in the Lord. But the reasons you give for doing so do not seem to me sufficient. It would be better for you to stay where you are and exhibit in a bishop the dress and holy life of a monk."[2] On the other hand whole communities of monks living outside their cloister and devoting themselves to the active apostolate would certainly have seemed to him at least incongruous. Certain monks might on occasion leave their cloister temporarily for a special mission, but he did not think that in the ordinary way this was the business of a monk. According to the traditional view the monastic vocation was something quite different from the priesthood and complete in itself. There were priests in monasteries but they were there for the spiritual needs of the community and they fulfilled the duties of their office by attending to the needs of their brethren. The modern custom of ordaining all choir monks as a matter of course, so that an impediment to the priesthood is also an impediment to monastic profession, has arisen from a new and different view of the monastic life.[3]

Nowadays we expect even the great men of the past to justify themselves in our eyes by their social teaching. But it would be idle to expect from Bernard any novel ideas on society; he was a child of the twelfth century and content to work within the feudal framework of his age. In his view it was irrelevant whether a man were rich or poor so long as he saved his soul. He saw nothing wrong in the possession of riches provided they had been acquired honestly and were used for the benefit of others. He thought that a man held his riches on trust from God for the benefit of himself and his neighbour. The poor were very dear to him because he regarded them as the special children of Christ, but it did not worry him that they

[1] Ep. 90 (Migne 87).
[2] Ep. 175 (Migne 319).
[3] The Church at Clairvaux consecrated in 1166 had 32 altars and each priest had his own, but there were more than four times that number of choir monks. Mass was not said every day by all the priests, and even as late as 1738 the General Chapter only expected monks to say Mass three or four times a week.

should be poor; he was poor himself and thought it did not signify greatly whether a man were rich or poor. No one was so obscure that he could not call on him for help and he always answered all his letters even from the most humble people.[1]

In addressing the great of this world on behalf of the poor he was quite fearless and did not hesitate to invoke divine sanctions. Thus when Conrad, Duke of Zeringen, was contemplating war against Amadeus I, Count of Geneva, Bernard wrote to him: "All power comes from him to whom the Prophet said: 'Thine, Lord, the power; of all princes art thou overlord.' So it seems fitting, illustrious Prince, that I should write and admonish Your Excellency to bow down before the terrible one who strikes with terror the hearts of princes. The Prince of Geneva has offered himself to justice and is ready to make satisfaction to you in all that you have against him. So if you set out to invade his territory, destroy churches, burn down homesteads, and shed human blood, there can be no doubt that you will seriously anger him who is 'the father of the orphan and gives the widow redress'. A poor man myself, I am stirred by the cries of the poor to write to you knowing full well that it would be more honourable for you to yield to a humble man than to submit to an enemy.... If you will neither receive the satisfaction offered to you nor listen to my entreaties, or rather, if you will not heed the voice of God warning you through me for the good of your soul, then may he be your judge."[2]

Bernard's letters to the Pope would astonish us nowadays by their bluntness. But in those days men had a clearer understanding of the distinction between the office and the man, and no one was considered beyond criticism by virtue of his office. Even quite insignificant people felt they could speak their minds of the highest clergy without incurring any suspicion of disloyalty, although it is true that open criticism of the folly or stupidity of those in high places was no more the royal road to preferment in Church or State then than it is now. Bernard took the supremacy of the Apostolic See completely for granted: "If you show the reverence that is due to the Apostolic See," he wrote to the people of Milan, "it will be a reverence without reserve, for the Apostolic See, by a unique privilege, is endowed with full authority over all the Churches of the world. Anyone who withstands this authority sets his face

[1] Ep. 235 to Bishop Buggo of Worms.
[2] Ep. 97 (Migne 97).

against the decrees of God."[1] A disciple of Hildebrand, he held
that the Holy See had two swords, the temporal and the spiritual.
"Without doubt," he wrote to Pope Eugenius III in his book on
Consideration, "the Church has two swords, a material and a
spiritual one. The first is to be used for her and the second by her."[2]
Again, writing to the same Pope on the sorry plight of the Church
in the East he said: "In this second passion of Christ we must draw
those two swords that were drawn during the passion. And who is
to draw them but you? Both of Peter's swords must be drawn
whenever necessary; the one by his command and the other by his
hand."[3]

Nevertheless Bernard did consider that since Hildebrand's day
the centralization of the Church had gone too far. He believed the
appeals to the court of Rome had become excessive and were used
more as an instrument for evading than for maintaining justice, and
he deplored the endless delays that these appeals involved. He did
not think the Curia was spotless or that the Cardinals were all without blemish; on the contrary he thought that both the system and the
personnel needed reform and that it was the duty of the Pope to
reform them.

In spite of the high tone Bernard sometimes took when he
addressed the great of this world, there is no doubt at all that he
was the most humble of men. Humility was his characteristic
virtue. Never on any occasion does he ever speak of himself except
in terms of complete disparagement, and there was no surer way of
annoying him than by praising him to his face. "You implore me,"
he writes to a friend, "to instruct you how you should live. Fine
sort of doctor, incomparable teacher that I am, who when I begin
to teach what I do not know may then be expected to realize at last
that I know nothing at all! A sheep might as well come to a goat
for wool as you to me for guidance. Furthermore in all your letters
you exalt me above myself, interlarding everything you say with
praises, praises which, as I am conscious I do not deserve them, I
must attribute to your good will while overlooking your ignorance
of the true facts . . . I put greater faith in what I see of myself than
I do in your praises who believe you see in me what I know is not
there."[4]

[1] Ep. 140 (Migne 131).
[2] De Consideratione Lib. 4, Ch. 3.
[3] Ep. 339 (Migne 256).
[4] Ep. 90 (Migne 87).

This letter is typical of many; there is hardly one in which he does not speak of himself as the greatest of sinners. But his humility was not merely a matter of words; even his opponents testified to his extreme modesty and self-effacing behaviour. He might have been anything had he so wished; there was no honour which he could not command; but he asked for nothing and refused everything he was offered. His only wish was to be left in peace in his monastery and that was the one thing he could not get! When all the world was hanging on his words, when the devout were giving him the veneration they usually reserve for their prophets when they have stoned them, Bernard never faltered in his firm belief that he was a useless vessel and the worst of sinners. But this did not mean that he could not defend his conduct when he found himself obstructed by the petty jealousy and narrow horizons of ecclesiastical bureaucrats and scandalmongers.

CHAPTER X

IN the year 1125 Hugh of Champagne relinquished his fief to his nephew Theobald, Count of Blois, and became a Knight of the Temple. This event was to have a far-reaching effect on the fortunes of both Bernard and his monastery, because, although there is some doubt about Bernard's relations with Count Hugh,[1] Theobald became one of his most powerful supporters. It is therefore no coincidence that Theobald's succession to the vast territory of Champagne should have coincided with a great improvement in the material position of Clairvaux and a vast extension of Bernard's influence.[2] His regard for Bernard and Bernard's influence over him was a matter of common knowledge if not of common envy, and also sometimes a source of embarrassment. Bernard's friendship and regard for the count was completely disinterested, but he very properly resented being approached by undeserving people as if he had had command over his friend's purse-strings. "The biting letter which, after your fashion, you have written to me, shows the wound in your own heart," he writes to one such person. "Whoever thinks," he continues, "that the count manages either himself or his estate by my advice cannot, I feel sure, know very well either the count or myself. . . . The count distributed his goods as he wished and to whom he wished. Some of his benefactions were made with my knowledge but not under my influence; perhaps I could have squeezed something out of him for myself had I so wished, but I thank God that, under his inspiration, I refused what he offered."[3] Nevertheless, he did not always refuse what the count offered, nor is

[1] But see Bernard's letter 32 (Migne 31).
[2] Theobald was related by blood to some of the greatest families in Europe and ruled a territory as large as, if not larger than, the kingdom of France. He was therefore well able to give Bernard all the support he might need from a layman. His early career seems to have been not very different from his own contemporaries and equals, but the shock of losing his sister and several of his family in the wreck of the White Ship in the year 1120 appears to have wrought a great change in him. He restrained his passions and turned his thoughts to the sobering truths of religion greatly to the benefit of the churches and clergy in his territory. He even considered becoming a monk but was dissuaded from doing so by St. Norbert. In the year 1126 he married Matilda the daughter of Englebert, Duke of Carinthia, and settled down to a life of piety as a Christian prince.
[3] Ep. 447 (Migne 416).

there any reason why he should have done so, and it was largely due to his generosity that Bernard was able to rebuild Clairvaux on a larger scale and in a more suitable position. But for the most part Bernard used his influence over his friend only to remind him of his duty towards God and man. Typical of many of Bernard's letters to him is one in which he asks him to show special favour to the Canons of Larzicourt who were in trouble with their neighbours, and then goes on to tell him about a poor woman he had met at Bar: "She implored me with tears to intercede for her, and my heart was moved to pity for her troubles. She is the wife of that man of yours Balin on whom you lately visited many great penalties for the evil he has done. Be merciful that you may obtain mercy." Then in one of those vivid pictures of the life of his times that make the study of his letters so rewarding he describes the wretched condition of an unfortunate man who had fought a duel in the presence of the count's prefect at Bar and had had his eyes put out and his property distrained as a consequence not of fighting the duel but of losing it, "as if," writes Bernard, "to have lost a duel and had his eyes put out were not enough without your servants taking away his property." Although clean contrary to the laws of the Church, duels and trials by fighting were in fact common enough at this time, and it would be too much to expect a man of Bernard's antecedents and background to be squeamish about them. He concludes this letter by reminding the count of his feudal duties: "I hope that you will show all honour to the bishops that have met in your capital [Troyes] to discuss matters that concern the glory of God. May you devoutly and obediently assist the Legate who has decided to honour both you and your city by holding there such a great council ... and may you receive the Bishop of Langres with special deference and render him reverently and humbly the homage you owe for the fief you hold from him."[1]

In the meantime Bernard's influence was growing outside his monastery. In the year 1125 he was asked to intervene between the canons of Châlons and their Bishop Ebal. There had been trouble over the election of a new superior. The majority of the canons had elected a man of great reforming zeal, but a few of them, dissenting strongly from the result of the election because they were quite out of sympathy with the candidate's views, chose a man more to their liking and persuaded the bishop to support them. A vig-

[1] Ep. 41 (Migne 39).

orous letter from Bernard to the bishop on behalf of the first candidate seems to have settled the affair in favour of the reforming party.

At Cambrai in the north of France Bernard made his influence felt by having an unsatisfactory abbot of St. Sepulchre removed in favour of another man better suited for the office. And in the year 1126 we find him writing to Pope Honorius in support of Alberic of Rheims who had been elected to the see of Châlons. For some reason the Pope had been withholding his confirmation of the election. But the time had not come when Bernard's lightest word was listened to with respect in Rome and Alberic had to remain at Rheims. He later became Archbishop of Bourges. Two years later Bernard was invited by the Bishop of Verdun to help in clearing up the scandal of the nuns at Laon. Their lives had not been edifying, and on Bernard's advice they were dispersed and their property handed over to monks. The abbot of the new community was called Drogo and may possibly have been the same Drogo of St. Nicasius who had tried his vocation at Pontigny.[1]

A scandal in the Court of the King, Louis the Fat, provided another occasion for Bernard to make his influence felt. The King had appointed as his Seneschal a certain Stephen de Garlande. The family of Garlande had enjoyed for more than a decade the confidence of the throne and Stephen had succeeded his brother William. The post of Seneschal carried with it command of the armed forces as well as attendance on the person of the King. But Stephen besides holding this post was also a deacon, Archdeacon of Notre Dame no less, and for good measure Dean of Orleans as well, and it was this that stuck in the throat of his contemporaries. A pluralist might be swallowed, but a pluralist who was also in command of the armed forces was too much. Bernard wrote a vigorous letter to his newly converted friend Suger, Abbot of St. Denis, who stood high in the councils of the King, imploring him to do all in his power to remove this "detestable impropriety". "What sort of monster is this," he asks, "that being a cleric wants to be a soldier as well, and succeeds in being neither?"[2] The scandal provided its own remedy, for Stephen, his head rather swollen by flattery and honours, made himself objectionable to the Queen and was promptly banished from the palace.

[1] V. sup., Ch. V.
[2] Ep. 80 (Migne 78).

It was inevitable that under the circumstances of those days the bishoprics should have been coveted and sometimes obtained by men who thought more of the temporal advantages of the office than the spiritual responsibilities. One of Bernard's earliest and most striking conversions in this sphere was of Henry Archbishop of Sens, not inappropriately surnamed the Wild Boar. This must have been some time before 1128 for in that year he dedicated to him a short treatise on the Conduct and Duty of Bishops, with a preface congratulating him on the good reports he had heard of him from "the most truthful lips of the Bishop of Meaux". In this short work Bernard, quite in the spirit of Hildebrand, enlarges on the responsibilities of a bishop and the need for him to be zealous in his pastoral work, charitable, and humble. He emphasizes that the great riches of a bishop's see are the patrimony of the poor and not for the luxurious living of the occupant. In a very typical passage he addresses a bishop through the mouth of the poor, saying: "Tell me, ye priests, what purpose has the gold on the bridles of your horses? Does gold feed the bridle or does it keep the bridle warm? We are famished and we are cold, but what good are all your cloaks and coats to us? Yet they are ours, they belong to us, and your wild expenditure is a robbery from us . . . you nourish your vanity at the expense of our necessity." But Bernard does not concern himself in this work wholly with bishops. In the last chapter he rounds on abbots and upbraids them for trying to obtain exemption from episcopal jurisdiction for their abbeys, and for acting the petty prelate with the ring and mitre of a bishop. This conclusion of Bernard's treatise on the duties of bishops has not received from scholarly monks the same close attention that they have devoted to the rest of the work.

About this time a quarrel flared up between the King and the Bishop of Paris. The origins of this trouble are obscure and the story becomes rather confused, but it only concerns us in so far as it involved Bernard. Bernard's exhortations had stirred the bishops of the province of Sens to take their pastoral duties more seriously. The Bishop of Paris, Stephen of Senlis, seems to have been one of the leaders in this reform. With the encouragement of Suger he set about trying to set the Chapter of Notre Dame in order. It need hardly be said that the canons objected to this; their way of life had become traditional and they did not see why they should change it. They appealed to the King, who was their patron, for his support and the King upheld their cause against the bishop, forbidding him to change in any way the long-established customs of the Chapter. The bishop, very conscious of his strong canonical position, ignored the King and went ahead with his reforms. The King promptly deprived him of his regalia and the bishop just as promptly replied by laying the whole diocese under an interdict. Feelings began to run high, violence broke out, and the bishop fled for his life to Sens taking refuge with the Archbishop. What had started by a private quarrel between the King of France and the Bishop of Paris now became an open fight between the whole party of reform and the throne. Under these circumstances it would have been impossible for Bernard to remain inactive; all his dearest principles were at stake. The whole Cistercian Order rallied behind him in defence of the Bishop of Paris and weighed in with a long letter of protest to the King. Apparently the King had asked for their prayers and had been admitted to an association of brotherhood with the Order, and in their letter to him the Cistercian Abbots ask why he should have sought association with their Order and a share in their prayers if he intended to alienate them and render their prayers for him of no avail by persecuting the Church in the person of the Bishop of Paris. They then go on to say that the bishop had asked for their support in an appeal to Rome but that they thought it better first to arrange a meeting with the King to see if an arrangement could be reached by peaceful means. It is a firm and very dignified letter, but to mention an appeal to Rome was a mistake for it put the idea into the King's head of getting in first at Rome and putting his version of the story to the Pope before he had heard the other side. However, some sort of meeting does appear to have been held and the King seemed on the point of giving way when a bombshell burst amongst the ranks of the Cistercians in the shape of a rescript from Rome supporting the King and over-ruling the interdict of the Bishop of Paris. At once the King's attitude hardened; he refused to discuss the matter any further and renewed his savage attack on the Bishop of Paris and his supporters. The situation now became dangerous and Bernard strode to the fore with a very strong and outspoken letter to the Pope. It is not clear how this wretched affair ended. It seems to have smouldered on for some time, every now and then flaring up in some outrageous incident like the murder of Thomas the Prior of St. Victor in Paris. But some sort of peace or truce seems to have been patched up.

When he saw that the Bishop of Paris with the backing of the Cistercians was too strong for him, the King turned on the Archbishop of Sens who, as we have seen, had lately joined the party of reform, and began to make covert suggestions that he had obtained his See by simony. "Who was the Archbishop of Sens to talk of reform and act the Saint? Was his position so unassailable? How had he acquired his See?" These were the questions the King began asking and there is no doubt that they were awkward and embarrassing questions for Archbishop Henry of Sens to answer. But the Cistercians with Bernard at their head rallied to the support of their new friend. "It is more zeal for righteousness, piety of life and religion itself in the persons of the bishops that the King is persecuting," wrote the abbots, doubtless at the dictation of Bernard, to Pope Honorius. Then in a letter signed only by himself Bernard writes to his friend Cardinal Haimeric, Chancellor to the Holy See, saying that when the Archbishop was leading a worldly life "ruled by the desires of the flesh," the King had nothing but praise for him, only after he had reformed did he begin to be persecuted; "and now," says Bernard, "they are looking for simony under the swaddling clothes of the child Jesus; their spiteful curiosity is probing the corpse of dead vice under new-born virtue."[1]

Unfortunately Henry's new-born virtue did not survive its swaddling clothes. His violent temperament could not be held in check for long, and in the end he gave his enemies ample pretext to compass his downfall. After a few years we find Bernard writing to him: "I confess that I have often intended to write to you for your own sake on behalf of others, and have then decided that it would be no use to do so on account of your hateful hardness . . . I want to keep your friends for you, but you will not condescend to it. I wish to reconcile your enemies to you, but you will not suffer it. You will not have peace, you are set on rushing to your shame, confusion, and destruction."[2] He was suspended in the year 1136 and six years afterwards, just before his death, he was deposed.

About this time the letters of Bernard begin to express his distress at being called out of his monastery so often to intervene in external affairs. Thus to the Cardinal Deacon Peter he writes: "It was not laziness, but a very much better reason that prevented me from

[1] Ep. 54 (Migne 51).
[2] Ep. 224 (Migne 182).

coming when you sent for me. The truth is, saving your reverence, and the reverence due to all good men, I have determined never to leave my monastery again except for certain reasons none of which could be invoked on this occasion as a pretext for satisfying your wishes and indeed my own."[1] There are many other letters in which he says the same thing, but peace and seclusion were never to be his lot.

It must not be thought that Bernard's activities were always appreciated. His prestige and fame had spread far beyond the confines of his own neighbourhood and even his own country, but his activities did not please everyone. It is natural that those whom he opposed should not be well disposed towards him, but there is evidence that at this time even some of those who should have been his allies regarded his activities outside the cloister unfavourably. Many of these people, no doubt good hearted and zealous clergymen within their own limitations, found his outspokenness difficult to understand or appreciate. He was not one of them; he did not (in the jargon of our day) belong to their trades union; he was a monk with a dominating personality and strong views about what did not directly concern him, and if they found his bluntness difficult to bear they must have found his prestige and success insupportable. It was inevitable that first whispers and then unmistakable complaints should eventually reach the Curia. Then one day a letter for Bernard arrived from his friend Cardinal Haimeric suggesting that he would do better to remain in his monastery and cease interfering in matters outside his monastery. Most unfortunately this letter has disappeared, probably it was destroyed, but we have his spirited reply and it is worth quoting for it is a classical example of how a truly great and humble man reacts when confronted with well-meaning but frustrating opposition from men smaller than himself. He comes to the point immediately: "Cannot wretchedness escape envy?" he asks. "Must truth always breed hatred even for the poor and needy? Should I regret or should I be glad that you treat me as an enemy? Is it because I spoke the truth or because I did right? This is for your dear brothers in Curia to decide who 'speak evil of the deaf' against the law and who, regardless of the Prophet's curse, 'call good evil and evil good'." Then after enumerating the various disputes in which he had been embroiled and the scandals which he had helped to remove, and after pointing out that he had

[1] Ep. 18 (Migne 17).

only intervened on the summons of the bishops, he goes on to say: "I am vexed at having been embroiled in these disputes, especially as I knew that I was not personally concerned. I am vexed but I am dragged into them none the less. But by whom can I better hope to be relieved of all this than by you, the best of men? You do not lack the power to do this and it is clear that you have the will. I am delighted to know that you are displeased that I should have been concerned in these affairs. It is most just and friendly of you. May it please you to bestir yourself in the matter, and because you understand that it is expedient for your friend and becoming for a monk, see that what we both want is speedily effected. . . . In this way perhaps your friend can avoid the stigma of presumption. Indeed I do not know how I was able to incur it, for I know it was my purpose and determination never, except on business of the Order, to leave my monastery unless the Legate of the Apostolic See or my own Bishop bade me do so. As you know very well, a person of my humble condition may not refuse the command of higher authorities. So if I can achieve this through your good offices, then without any doubt I shall have peace at home and leave others at peace. But I do not think that because I am hidden away and keeping silent the troubles of the Church will cease, at any rate so long as the Curia continues to pass judgements to the prejudice of the absent in order to gratify those who are at hand. Farewell."[1] And so Bernard was able to stay in his monastery undisturbed, and well content he was that this should be so. But the time was at hand when enormous disaster would force him to come forth again, and this time it would be not to remove some local scandal but to save the Church itself from shipwreck.

[1] Ep. 51 (Migne 48).

CHAPTER XI

St. Norbert, the founder of the Premonstratensians and Archbishop of Magdeburg, was sure that he would live to see the coming of Antichrist and a general persecution of the Church, but Bernard did not agree. Writing of a visit he had paid to Norbert he said: "He spoke of the coming of Antichrist and declared himself quite certain that it would be during the present generation. But when he told me the reasons for his certainty I did not feel compelled to agree with him. He concluded by saying that he would live to see a general persecution of the Church."[1] Nevertheless Norbert was right and, for once, Bernard was mistaken. Early in the Spring of 1130 the appalling news reached Clairvaux, not improbably from Norbert himself, that two Popes were claiming the Chair of Peter and were ready to tear the Church in half to satisfy their ambitions. On one and the same day and within a few hours the Roman people had acclaimed as Pope both the Cardinal Deacon Gregory of S. Angelo and the Cardinal Priest Peter Leon.

The origins of this unhappy affair seem to have had their roots in a decree by Pope Nicolas II. Previously the prerogative of electing a new Pope rested primarily with the cardinal priests and deacons, who were known simply as the cardinals, and the cardinal bishops had only to confirm the result of the election and consecrate the candidate. But in the year 1059 Pope Nicolas decreed that when a pope died the responsibility of electing his successor should rest first with the cardinal bishops, and that after they had made their choice and before submitting him to the clergy and people of Rome for approval, they should associate themselves with the cardinal clerks. Unfortunately two versions of this decree were current, the original and a corrupt version in which the operative word "bishops" had been left out so as to give the impression that the cardinal clerks had at least as much say in the election of a pope as the cardinal bishops. This alone would have been enough to ensure trouble and confusion, but when to this is added the seething condition of Rome owing to the antagonism of the Pierleoni and the Frangipani, two

[1] Ep. 59 (Migne 56).

99

powerful families who divided the city into opposing camps, trouble and confusion were inevitable.

The Pierleoni had a candidate for the papacy in the person of Peter Leon, the cardinal priest of SS. Cosmas and Damian. Even if we discount the allegations of his enemies it is hard to find anything good to say of this man. The son of a converted Jew who had in one way and another amassed a huge fortune, he had started his career as a monk of Cluny. After he had been raised to the Sacred Purple he was sent for a time to England as the pope's Legate, where he seems to have made important friends, no doubt with an eye to the future. Clearly he was a man of considerable resource and ability, but this appears to be all that can be said for him. Even his friends seem to have found it hard to discover anything better to say of him. He was a man utterly devoured by ambition and quite unscrupulous about how he achieved his goal. Peter the Venerable, usually so moderate in his statements, describes him as guilty of "ambition, perjury, cupidity, and yet worse", and Peter the Venerable should have known, for Peter Leon had been a monk of his community. Very early in his career he seems to have set his heart on obtaining the papal tiara for himself. His great riches and the enormous influence of his family were enough to bring it within his grasp. As soon as it became evident that Pope Honorius had not much longer to live, Peter Leon began to manœuvre towards his goal. But he had to contend with the Chancellor, Cardinal Haimeric. Haimeric did not covet the tiara for himself, but seems to have been a high-minded man, intent only on saving the Church from the greedy ambitions of the Pierleoni. When he saw what was afoot he moved the ailing pontiff out to the monastery of St. Andrew on the Coelian[1] in an endeavour to assure that the election of his successor should be untrammelled by external pressure. This was on 10th February, 1130. From now on the whole affair becomes confused by a mass of conflicting evidence, but what seems to have happened was this. On 11th February Haimeric summoned all the cardinals out to St. Andrew's to discuss what action had best be taken to ensure a free election. All the cardinals agreed that if anyone should attempt to elect a new pope before the burial of Honorius, he would be *ipso facto* excommunicated. At the suggestion of Cardinal William of Palestrina a rider was added to the effect that anyone who tried to elect a second pope should also be anathema.

[1] Now the Church of St. Gregory on the Coelian.

At this Peter Leon shouted out that he for one would never dream of doing such a thing, that he would rather be drowned before inflicting such a scandal on the Church. It may be added that by Canon Law no election might be held until the Pope had been buried and until three days after his death. The next day, 12th February, all the cardinals met again and decided to entrust the election to eight of their number: Peter the Red, Peter Leon, and Peter of Pisa, cardinal priests; and Gregory of St. Angelo, Jonathan, and Haimeric, cardinal deacons. After this had been more or less peacefully decided the first signs of trouble began with the cardinal bishops refusing to part with the key of the Church of St. Adrian near the capital, where it had been decided to hold the election. The cardinals Peter and Jonathan left in a rage and the meeting arranged for the next day did not take place, but a rumour was spread abroad, probably by the supporters of Peter Leon, that Pope Honorius had died. In order to calm the excited mob that had gathered round St. Andrew's, the sick pontiff had to show himself at the window of the monastery. Exhausted by this effort he died the same evening. Now Haimeric acted with a promptitude that does him credit, but in a manner that only the unfortunate circumstances could excuse. A free election would have been impossible if the news had once got abroad that the Pope was dead. Rome was boiling. The Pierleoni had armed their followers and scattered gold to increase their number. Therefore very early in the morning Haimeric summoned the cardinals to St. Andrew's without mentioning what had happened. Fourteen came, four cardinal bishops, five cardinal priests, and four cardinal deacons including Haimeric himself. Amongst these cardinals there were six of the original committee of eight who had been entrusted with the election. But Peter Leon and Jonathan were not there. They had already begun to hatch their own schemes. As soon as the cardinals had arrived and learnt the news they decided to act at once. So as to observe at least the letter of the law, which they had made themselves two days ago, they buried the dead Pope in a temporary tomb. Having done this they set about electing his successor in the teeth of the law which forbade an election to be held within three days of a pope's death. The only one to have any misgivings about this proceeding was Peter of Pisa; he refused to take any part in it and left to join the party of Peter Leon and acquaint them of what was on foot. He seems to have been an honest and even scrupulous man, one of the very few such men to support the rival pope. His defection was undoubtedly serious, but it still left five out of the original committee of eight. The election went forward and ended in the unanimous choice of Gregory; there had been no time to waste and no time had been wasted, as at any moment the Pierleoni might have broken in. After a brief hesitation Gregory accepted the result of the election and was promptly hustled off to the Lateran by Haimeric, and there acclaimed by the populace as Pope Innocent II. He was then hurried away to the Palladium on the Palatine, near the stronghold of the Frangipani, where he was invested with the insignia of his office. Then the storm burst. The Pierleoni and their supporters in a frenzied rage at being outwitted by Haimeric rushed to the church of St. Mark to hold another election. The hole-and-corner nature of the first election and its obvious irregularity, gave Peter Leon the pretext for which he had been waiting. Soon the church was filled with a vast crowd, amongst whom were only two cardinal bishops, but thirteen cardinal priests, nine cardinal deacons, and a large number of bishops, priests and nobility. Here was an excellent opportunity for the cardinal priests and deacons to assert their pretended prerogatives in the election of a Pope and the result could not have been otherwise than it was. With one accord they all chose Peter Leon, their patron, as the true successor of Pope Honorius. Peter, Bishop of Porto, invested him with the papal insignia (doubtless duplicates were kept for just such emergencies) and by midday the populace, which three hours before had acclaimed Gregory as Pope Innocent II, were ready to do the same for Peter Leon and acclaim him as Pope Anacletus. The following day Peter, in his new role as Vicar of Christ, started out at the head of a vast rabble to grab his rival from the hands of the Frangipani and, when this proved impossible, to invest the basilicas of St. Peter and the Lateran. Here his arms met with better success, for he was able to capture both these sacred buildings and plunder them to his heart's content, and with the vast spoils thus acquired buy up the support of nearly everyone in Rome. On 23rd February, nine days after the elections, a lull in hostilities enabled both Popes to be consecrated, Innocent by the Bishop of Ostia in Santa Maria Novella and Anacletus by the Bishop of Porto in Saint Peter's. Then, the ceremonies and formalities over, both proceeded to hurl anathemas at each other and to descend once again to more effective if less becoming methods of pulling each other down, but it should be said that in all this sorry business Gregory seems to have behaved with laudable restraint and never once to have resorted to arms except in self-defence. Finally, the support of his friends having become ineffective, he left Rome altogether and sailed for France. A man of peace and a pious man, he was at a certain disadvantage when faced with his unscrupulous adversary, but as things turned out he could not have done better than leave Rome. True, he left his rival in possession but as yet only Rome acknowledged him. The Emperor Lothair and the Kings of the West had not yet spoken and Innocent had gone out to meet them. Had the situation been reversed and Anacletus been turned from Rome leaving Innocent in possession, the conclusion of the struggle might also have been reversed to the great misfortune of the Church.

There is no doubt that the election of Gregory had been highly irregular and it is impossible to escape the impression that Haimeric had acted in a high-handed and clandestine manner, but the supporters of Gregory alleged, and not without reason, that Haimeric was justified in acting as he did by the exceptional circumstances of the situation. With Rome in the seething condition that it was a free election would not have been possible by the normal procedure and we must also take into account that Haimeric appears to have done all in his power to secure the co-operation of Peter Leon. However irregular the election of Gregory may have been, the election of Anacletus was plainly illicit. It was a second election held with a cynical disregard of the first without any attempt to prove it invalid. It is true that Peter seems to have had on his side the majority of the cardinals, but it is equally true that Gregory had the votes of all the more reputable and responsible of them as well as a majority of the committee to whom the election had been entrusted with the consent of Peter himself. Furthermore Peter forfeited all claim to any consideration that he might have had by his violent and brutal behaviour after his election. Whatever his limitations, Gregory was unquestionably a man of real piety and unblemished good name whereas, as Bernard characteristically remarks, the reputation of his rival was not safe even amongst his friends.

Neither Bernard nor Peter the Venerable seems to have had the slightest hesitation in accepting Innocent as the true Pope. Undoubtedly the superiority of Innocent's character over that of his rival weighed very heavily with Bernard, we could hardly expect it to have been otherwise, and in this he had the authority of Yves, the saintly and learned Bishop of Chartres, who held that when an election was in dispute the more popular and virtuous candidate should be preferred.[1] But this was not Bernard's only reason for supporting Innocent; he was far too clear a thinker to believe that his blameless life was in itself a convincing argument for the validity of his election. "Whether we like it or not," he wrote to the Bishops of Aquitaine, "the truth of the Holy Spirit must be fulfilled; the scandals foretold in the Scriptures must come to pass. But woe to the man through whom they come! It would have been better for him had he never been born. And who else can he be but the man of sin who, notwithstanding that a Catholic had been canonically elected by Catholics, invaded the holy place, not because it was a holy place but just because it was the highest place. He invaded it, I say, and he invaded it with arms, fire, and bribes, not at all by the merits and virtues of his life. And he has arrived there and stands there by the same means that brought him there. The election of his supporters of which he makes so much was not an election but a faction, a mere shadow and excuse, a cover for his malice. It could be called a sort of election, but it would be an impudent lie. The authentic decree of the Church still holds: after the one election there cannot be another. When one election has taken place, a second is not an election at all, it is utterly null and utterly void. Even if the first election did take place with less solemnity and order than the second, as the enemies of unity contend, how can anyone have presumed to hold another without first discussing the manner of the former and suppressing it by a considered judgement?"[2]

But the Church in France did not at once follow the lead of Bernard and Peter the Venerable. It prudently suspended judgement, and the King himself was a little doubtful, for Anacletus was a personal friend of his. It is very much to the credit of Louis that he did not attempt to adjudicate on the matter himself; instead he called a council of the chief ecclesiastics of his realm to meet at Etampes and there to decide the question, and he personally invited Bernard.

Bernard must have been torn in two by this invitation from the

---

[1] Panormia. Pat. Lat. 161, 1130: ". . . is alteri praeferatur qui majoribus studiis juvatur et meritis." Vacandard: Via de S. Bernard, Vol. 1, p. 304 (1927), translated *majoribus studiis* as "le plus de partisans".

[2] Ep. 129 (Migne 126).

King. On the one hand he had been strongly advised, if not ordered, by the highest authority to remain in his monastery and not to meddle in affairs outside his Order, and on the other hand the Church seemed to be in jeopardy and appealing to him for the help which he must have known he could give. He was a monk heart and soul, but as we have seen he was also a man of the Church; it would have been against his nature and against his destiny to refuse the King's invitation and remain peacefully in his cloister however much he must have wished to do so. He must have been conscious of his special gifts, and special gifts imply a special vocation. And so he made his choice, set out for Etampes, and said good-bye for ever to the secluded life of peace and prayer for which his whole soul yearned, and which he had purchased as a young man at so great a price. The day would come when he would be writing to the Carthusian Prior of Portes: "May my monstrous life, my bitter conscience, move you to pity. I have become a sort of modern chimaera, neither cleric nor layman. I have kept the tonsure of a monk, but I have long ago abandoned the life."[1] If this was disobedience, never did a man disobey more reluctantly; if this was disobedience, it was that inspired disobedience we occasionally find in the lives of the Saints, parallel to the disobedience of Nelson when he refused to withdraw from battle at the command of his superior officer. We are told that on the way to Etampes he was heartened by a vision foretelling the success of his efforts to unite the Church. It may be true, there is no evidence to the contrary, but it does not seem the way that God works when He deals with His great lovers. More often He seems to test their courage to the utmost by leaving them in darkness and obscurity. This was the second and final turning point in the life of Bernard when the ways parted before him and he had to choose: first when as a youth he had given up his career to serve God in the cloister, and now when he refused the peace of the cloister in order to serve the Church in the turmoil of the world. On both occasions he might have acted differently for reasons both plausible and prudent, and had he done so no one could have blamed him and there would have been many to praise him. Yet it is not too much to say that the history of the world would have been different and the loss to the Church, humanly speaking, incalculable. It needed great courage for him to enter Citeaux, but courage of a far higher type was needed for him to

[1] Ep. 326 (Migne 250).

come to the aid of the Church at this crisis when he might so easily have remained aloof within the secure precincts of his monastery under the universally applauded pretext of obedience.

When the council met it was agreed that the question of the validity of the two elections was too nice a point and too open to subtle dispute and disquisition to carry the necessary conviction or to form a solid basis on which to build a firm policy. It was determined instead to let the whole question depend on which of the two rivals was the better man. When this had been agreed upon it seemed clear to everyone that there could be no one better able to judge such a matter than Bernard the man of God. We have no record of what he said when he addressed the council, but we have already seen what he thought of Anacletus and he mentions him again in a letter to Hildebert the Archbishop of Tours in words perhaps not so very different from those he used at Etampes: "I will speak to you in the words of the Prophet," he wrote, "and I will say 'Comfort is hidden from mine eyes because death hath divided the brethren'. For it seems to me that, according to Isaias, they have made a covenant with death and a compact with hell. Innocent, the anointed of the Lord, has been set up for the fall and rise of many. Those who are of God have freely chosen him, but he who stands over against him is either Antichrist or his disciple. The abomination of desolation is standing in the Holy Place, to gain possession of which he has set fire to the sanctuary of God. He persecutes Innocent and with him all who are innocent. Innocent has fled from his face, for 'when the lion roars who shall not be afraid'?[1] He has obeyed the words of the Lord himself: 'When they persecute you in one city flee unto another.' He has fled and by the flight that he has endured after the example of the Apostles, he has shown himself really an apostle."[2] As we should expect Bernard's eloquence won a complete triumph for Innocent and Suger was sent at once to take the good news to him at Cluny, where he was staying at the time.

The King of France had submitted to Innocent, but the King of England still hesitated. As we have seen, Anacletus had spent some time in England and had made powerful friends there. Bernard met the King somewhere in his territory on the continent. "What are you doubtful about?" he asked him when the King still seemed to

---

[1] "Leo rugiet, quis non timebit," a quotation from Amos III, 8, and a play on the name of Peter Leon.
[2] Ep. 127 (Migne 124).

hesitate. "Is it that you are afraid of sinning by submitting to Innocent? Well, you just think of your other sins and leave this one to me. I will answer for it." After this the King submitted. He had not often been spoken to like that.

When Suger arrived at Cluny with the news that the King and the Church in France had recognized his claim to the papal tiara, Innocent set out at once for Clermont, where he celebrated the occasion by once more launching anathemas at his rival, without, however, inflicting any very noticeable harm on him so far as we can judge. Then near Orleans he received the formal submission of the King of France and all his court. At Chartres the King of England came forward to make his obeisance offering rich presents to the Pope and even persuading the Jews to do the same. It seems strange that the Jews should have felt so strongly on the issue as to be willing to part with any of their wealth, but we are not told what means the King took to persuade them.

When Innocent had been at Clermont messengers had arrived to inform him that the Emperor Lothair had recognized his claim in a council held at Wurtzburg, so he arranged to meet him and his court at Liége during the spring of the following year. Bernard accompanied him and it was as well that he did so, for, after the first formal courtesies, Lothair, who seems to have been listening to bad advice, repudiated the concordat of Worms and made it quite clear that his recognition of Innocent would depend on the restoration to himself of the right to invest the bishops of his realm with the cross and ring. If his demand were refused, he made it very clear what would happen: the schism would come to a sudden and unfortunate end, for Innocent was in his power. Everyone seems to have been completely cowed except Bernard who leapt to his feet and upbraided the enraged Emperor to his face and before all his court on his disgraceful behaviour. Some time later, when the schism was all over, Bernard reminds Innocent of this incident in one of his letters to him: "And at Liége," he writes, "a choleric and furious king was unable to enforce, with his menacing sword, acquiescence to his shocking and shameless demands."[1] Bernard seems to have enjoyed piling up adjectives.

After his adventure at Liége Innocent lost no time in returning to France in order to spend Holy Week at St. Denis. Suger has left us an account of all the celebrations that marked this event; of the

[1] Ep. 155 (Migne 150).

great procession and of the songs by which the Pope was welcomed; of the sumptuous festivities on Maundy Thursday and of the even more magnificent ceremonies on Easter Day when the Pope and his entourage "multo et mirabili ornatu seipsos circumdantes" processed on horseback and in gorgeous apparel to the Abbey.[1]

The celebrations at St. Denis over, Innocent set out for Clairvaux travelling by Auxerre. Here a very different sort of welcome awaited him. Arnold of Bonneval strains all his resources of rhetoric to describe this edifying spectacle of the Pope being welcomed by the Poor of Christ at Clairvaux. Clichés roll from his pen like shot from a cartridge. "The Pope was met," he tells us, "not in purple and fine linen, but by serried ranks of the Poor of Christ in rags carrying a wooden cross; not with holy mirth but with restrained affection." The Pope and the cardinals and bishops all wept, which must have been rather embarrassing for everyone, but perhaps no one noticed, for Arnold tells us that everyone (except obviously Arnold himself) kept their eyes fixed on the ground. The only ornaments to be seen amidst those bare walls were the virtues of the monks: "There was nothing to move the greed of a Roman." Apparently the feast provided was a feast more of virtue than of food, but the Pope seems to have been given a little fish. Everyone, even the Cardinals, was edified, but their stay does not seem to have been so prolonged as it had been at Cluny and St. Denis.

After Clairvaux Innocent set out for Rheims to consolidate his success with a council convoked of five kingdoms, and Bernard went with him. The council opened in October with a requiem for Philip the heir to the throne of France, who had lately met with a fatal accident. While riding in the suburbs of Paris he was thrown by a pig, a "diabolico porco" running between his horse's legs.[2] The requiem was followed by the consecration of his younger brother Louis le Jeune as the future King of France. England, France, Castile, Aragon, and Germany were represented and letters of submission were presented from Lothair by the hand of Norbert, from Alphonsus I of Aragon and Alphonsus II of Castile by the bishops whom they had sent to represent them. Then to mark the occasion Innocent launched a fourth and final excommunication against his rival. It was a great day of triumph for Innocent, but his victory was still far from complete.

[1] Suger, Vita Ludovico Grossi. Pat. Lat. 186.1331.
[2] Suger ibid.

CHAPTER XII

In the Spring of 1132 Innocent set out for Italy leaving Bernard behind to win over those who still opposed him in France, notably Gerard of Angoulême, a man of high mettle and great intelligence, who, as the Apostolic Legate under four successive Popes, had served the Church well in Aquitaine. The only bishop stout enough to call the redoubtable William Count of Poitiers to book when he took to living in adultery, he was also one of the very few men who seem able to have resisted the magnetism of Bernard's personality. His ascendancy over Count William was complete and it was largely due to his influence that Aquitaine remained a centre of disaffection. It is difficult not to admire Gerard, but his character was marred by an ambition so inordinate and childish that it finally wrecked his career. In a letter to the Bishops of Aquitaine, whom Count William at the instigation of Gerard had been persecuting for their allegiance to Innocent, Bernard tells us how this came about: "That Diotrephas,[1] who covets pre-eminence amongst you, has not accepted you and does not recognize him whom the whole Church, together with you, has received as coming in the name of the Lord. And no wonder! For even at his time of life he craves for a great name. In remarking the vanity of this man, I am not being led away by false or uncertain reports; I am judging him by his own words. In a confidential letter he lately wrote to the chancellery he obsequiously and unworthily begged to be honoured with the prestige and burden of legate. Would that he had got it! Perhaps if his ambition had been satisfied, he would have hurt you less than he does now that it has been frustrated. He would only have harmed himself. Now he rages against the whole world. You see what love of glory can do! The office of legate is a burden even to more youthful shoulders than his. All the world knows this. Yet here is a very old man who finds it an agony to spend even the few days that are left to him without this burden. . . . The first thing he did, or one of the first things, after the election of Pope Innocent, was to write and beg for the legateship. When this was refused him, in his rage he turned against Innocent and went over to the other

[1] Gerard of Angoulême.

man, pluming himself on becoming his legate. If he had not asked for the legateship from Pope Innocent, or if he had afterwards refused to accept it from the other man, I might have believed that he had some other motive for his double-dealing, although it could not have been a good one. But now he has no excuse for his ambition. Let him lay aside the legateship which he now enjoys, although it is only an empty name without any substance, and I, if I can, will cease to suspect him or, if I cannot prevent myself, I will, at any rate, do so unwillingly and accuse myself of rashness in doing so. He is a man who has for so long lorded it over others that he is ashamed to hold any place but the first . . .

"It was because of this and nothing more that this man left him whom he once called 'Holy Father Innocent' and his holy mother the Church to cleave unto his schismatic, so that they became two in one vanity. They are men in love with themselves. They support each other in seeking their own interests and (what is shocking) they do so at the expense of Christ's heritage. . . . Even now the legate wants new bishops for his Pope, so that he shall not be alone in his support of him. He does not wait until the sees become vacant by death, but, supported by tyrannical power, he intrudes men into sees while the bishops are still alive, taking the spite of secular princes as an opportunity for this.

"We must not think that all this activity of the legate on behalf of his Pope is disinterested. He boasts that he has added the whole of France and Burgundy to his legatine jurisdiction. If he wants he can add Media, Persia, and the coasts of Decapolis! A man as stupid as he is conceited."[1]

So that was Gerard Bishop of Angoulême. He continued obstinately playing his losing game until, excommunicated and discredited, he died—some say suddenly and unshriven, others that on his death-bed he confessed and repented. But it was to be another two years before this happened and in the meantime his influence over Count William was supreme and wholly in favour of the anti-Pope. It was this that made him dangerous; alone, just as Bishop of Angoulême, Gerard could have done very little, but his patron ruled a territory as large as that of the King of France.

There is little that can be said in favour of Count William; weak, sensual and violent, he had none of Gerard's redeeming qualities. But if he could be weaned from Gerard's influence there

[1] Ep. 129 (Migne 126).

was every hope that he might be brought over to the side of Innocent. Bernard, having endeavoured in vain to approach him through the Duke of Burgundy, set out for Poitiers with the Bishop of Soissons to see what he could achieve in a personal interview. In this, as we should expect, he was more successful; the count, completely won over by Bernard's personality, agreed at once to support Innocent and break with Gerard, but only to relapse under Gerard's influence to his old behaviour as soon as Bernard's back was turned. "Contrary to everyone's expectations and much to everyone's delight," Bernard wrote to him, "I was able to bring away from you an assurance of your peaceful intentions towards the Church. But now I hear you have not scrupled to arouse the wrath of God against you, even more than before, by expelling the clergy of St. Hilary from their city, greatly to the harm of the Church. . . . Turn back, I pray you, turn back, or you will be cut off. Turn back, I say, and restore peace to your friends and their church to the clergy, or you will alienate irrevocably him that 'is feared by awestruck princes, feared amongst the kings of the earth'."[1] Count William's only reply to this was to turn with greater fury against the adherents of Innocent in his territory, expel the Bishop of Poitiers from his see, and smash the altar stone on which Bernard had said Mass. Gerard was always at hand to see that no letter from Bernard should influence him.

In the meantime things had not been prospering for Innocent in Italy. Rome was still beyond his grasp and he had been obliged to settle at Pisa for the time being. Everything was in a turmoil. Roger of Sicily was preparing to attack him on land and sea, and to meet this threat he desperately needed the help of the Genoese, but the Genoese had been quarrelling, off and on, with the Pisans for the last fifty years and nothing could persuade them to join forces in defence of the Pope or anyone else. It remained to summon Bernard to Italy and ask him to arbitrate between them; if he could do nothing no one could. So Bernard came to Italy and with his coming passions immediately began to subside: men felt his presence even if they did not meet him. He describes the success of his mission to the Genoese in a letter he wrote to them some time later: "My mission to you last year was not fruitless, as the Church, in whose service I came, was to discover in the hour of her need. You received me with honour and you tried to persuade me to stay

[1] Ep. 130 (Migne 128).

longer. This was more than a man in my humble sphere deserved, but it did you credit, and I have not forgotten it and am not ungrateful. . . . What joyous days those were, I only wish I could have stayed longer! Never shall I forget you, O faithful people, noble race, glorious state of Genoa! 'I cried aloud and made my plea known to you' and your readiness to listen was only matched by my love of the listeners. I brought to you words of peace and, finding you the sons of peace, I left my peace with you. I experienced no difficulty or delay, but almost on one and the same day I both sowed and reaped."[1] In March of the same year the people of Genoa and Pisa signed a peace accepting all the terms that Bernard proposed and agreeing to unite in defence of Pope Innocent. Within a few weeks of his arrival in Italy Bernard had established harmony amongst the quarrelling allies and eliminated all danger from the threats of Roger of Sicily.

Soon after this the Emperor Lothair arrived in Italy at the head of a small army and met Innocent at Viterbo. With his arrival an awkward situation developed which Bernard was called upon to save. Anacletus, feeling that his prospects of success were on the wane and, with good reason, fearful of the consequences of defeat, made the cunning move of sending ambassadors to Lothair with the suggestion that both elections should be submitted to the judgement of a council. Lothair, who seems to have been getting rather tired of the whole business, was inclined at first to favour the proposal, but Bernard would have none of it. "This is a mere subterfuge," he said. "What else is there for them to do, what else can they do better calculated to confuse the simple, arm the evilly disposed and palliate their own malice? What else but this could they say? But God has already judged the case which man is trying to re-open too late, and he has judged it by the evidence of the facts, not by the wording of some decree. 'His word runs swift' in bringing the people and kings together in one that they may serve and obey Pope Innocent. Who can appeal against this? . . .

"Are not the kings and princes of the world united in the same spirit together with their peoples, acclaiming Innocent and confessing that he is the pope and bishop of their souls? What man is there of good repute and illustrious in any rank of life who does not believe the same? Having been over-hasty in their election these people are endeavouring to re-open the case in order to have their

[1] Ep. 131 (Migne 129).

position confirmed. Now they are prepared to offer a tardy justice which they had the opportunity of doing at the proper time, so that if you now refuse they will appear to have right on their side, and if you accept something may turn up favourable to them during the delay caused by the disputes of the two parties . . .

"Let us grant, for the sake of argument, that God may change his decision, call together a council from the ends of the earth, and suffer the matter to be judged twice over. Whom, in such a case, would they choose as judges? All have taken sides in the matter and would not easily agree upon a judgement. Such a council would be rent by faction and lead to even more quarrelling rather than to peace. Then I would like to know to whom that schismatic would entrust Rome which, after he had desired it for so long, he has at last got into his clutches at great labour and expense, and which he possesses with such pride and would be ashamed to lose. If he should lose his suit but not his city the whole world would have assembled for nothing.

"The question is this: which of these two men seems to be the Pope? There is a great difference between the two persons but, so as not to seem to flatter or abuse either, I will simply say what you will find being said everywhere, namely that the character of Innocent and his good name need fear no comparison with that of his adversary, while his is not safe even amongst his friends. Then if you examine the elections you will at once see that ours is the more honest, more creditable, and the first in time."[1] That disposed of Anacletus. After this there was nothing else for the Emperor to do than to set off for Rome and try to turn him out.

"We are on the threshold of the city, delivery is at the gates, justice is on our side; but the Roman soldiers cannot live on such fare,"[2] wrote Bernard to King Henry I of England, but no help came from that quarter. Lothair's army was encamped on the Aventine, Innocent was safe in the Lateran, and the Genoese had come up the river, but the anti-Pope and his allies were in possession of St. Peter's and nothing would induce them to come out of their strongholds to give battle. A complete impasse ensued, for Lothair had not the forces to storm the citadels of the enemy; amid the narrow streets and tortuous alleys of medieval Rome they were far too strongly entrenched to be ejected and far too cunning to venture

[1] Ep. 129 (Migne 126).
[2] Ep. 141 (Migne 138).

forth. All the time trouble was brewing for Lothair in Germany from his rival Conrad of Hohenstaffen and the heats of summer were approaching with their threat of disease for his armies. Finally he decided to be crowned in the Lateran and then return immediately to Germany. Very soon after this Bernard also departed, leaving Innocent in the Lateran protected by the Frangipani.

"What can I say of the Roman people, save that they are the people of Rome?" he wrote some years later to another pope, his disciple Eugenius III. "I can think of nothing worse to say about them than this, for everyone knows of the pride and arrogance of these Romans. They are a people addicted to strife and unaccustomed to peace; a people both hot-headed and seditious, incapable of submission except when they lack the means to resist."[1] Clearly his short stay in the Eternal City had left a deep impression.

There was to be no rest for Bernard in France, for hardly had he got back to Clairvaux, if indeed he ever got as far, before he was overtaken by messengers from the Pope commanding him to arbitrate in a local schism that had broken out at Tours. As soon as the see had fallen vacant by the death of Hildebert in 1133, Geoffrey, Count of Tours, for reasons known only to himself, expelled the canons from the city, and when the Chapter had eventually found somewhere to meet a small party of them, elected quite uncanonically, in opposition to the candidate of the majority, a young monk of Fontaines-les-Blanches, by the name of Philip, a nephew of Hildebert's predecessor, Gilbert. At this point Bernard intervened with a personal appeal to Philip whom he seems to have known well. "You are causing me great sorrow, dearest Philip," he wrote; "I beg you not to mock at my grief, because, if you do not see why I should grieve for you, then there is all the more reason why I should do so. Whatever you think of yourself, I think that your condition calls for a whole fount of tears. My sorrow has no mere human cause, it is not occasioned by the loss of any perishable chattels, but of you, Philip. I cannot better describe how great is the cause of my sorrow than by saying that Philip is the cause of it."[2] But by the time this letter was written Philip had already left to have his election confirmed by the anti-Pope, and afterwards he returned to Tours to take possession of his see. In the meantime the candidate of the majority had been consecrated at Le Mans and Philip fled

[1] Ep. 141 (Migne 138).
[2] Ep. 157 (Migne 151).

from Tours taking with him all the treasure. Bernard called a meeting of the whole Chapter and after consulting with both sides advised the Pope to annul the election of Philip. Whereupon Philip fled again to the anti-Pope and his supporters appealed over Bernard's head to Innocent. At this Bernard immediately wrote to Innocent, "It is necessary that the church of Tours should be immediately succoured. Unless you bring it speedy aid, she will perish."[1] But Philip did not attempt to return, and the anti-Pope gave him the Archbishopric of Taranto to console him. This story has a happy ending, for Philip repented of his misdeeds and became a monk at Clairvaux where he was prior in 1153 when Bernard died.

Still no peace for Bernard; hardly had the business at Tours been settled when trouble bubbled up at Troyes. "The insolence of the clergy is being everywhere a nuisance and upsetting the whole Church," he wrote to Innocent. Immediately on the heels of this yet another and quite appalling catastrophe occurred. Stephen of Senlis, the Bishop of Paris, was returning from doing some good work with Thomas, the young Prior of the canons of St. Victor whom Stephen had installed in the Chapter of Notre-Dame, when, as they were passing the château of Stephen de Garlande at Gournay-sur-Marne, armed men rushed out and stabbed Thomas to death, even threatening the bishop. The young canon died in his bishop's arms. Instead of continuing on his way to Paris Stephen at once fled to Clairvaux and poured forth his story to Bernard. The wretched affair had its roots in the reforms which Thomas had been trying to introduce in the ecclesiastical courts. They had become hopelessly corrupt; it was impossible for anyone to obtain justice at them without bribing the Archdeacon Theobald Notier. This Notier, foreseeing that his pocket would suffer, had been strenuously fighting the reforms of Thomas and had threatened to have him murdered, a threat which he was able and ready to carry out.

As soon as he heard the story of the bishop Bernard at once wrote to Innocent. There were rumours that Notier was on his way to Rome to seek absolution from the Pope on the grounds that he was not personally guilty of the murder. "A wild beast has devoured Joseph," he cried to Innocent, "and, unable to meet the attacks of the dogs, it has fled to you for protection. The wretch must be mad to think that he, a wanderer and fugitive on earth, can find refuge where he should have most cause to fear. The scoundrel! Does he

[1] Ep. 155 (Migne 150).

think the seat of supreme justice is a den of thieves or a lair of lions? Does he seek refuge with the mother whose son he has butchered, does he dare to appear before the father, still licking his chops, his jaws still red with the blood of their son? . . . Do you ask, you wretch, 'Was it I that killed him?' No, not you, it is true, but your people on your account. Whether by your designs or not, God will see and judge. If you have any excuse, you whose teeth are spears and arrows, you whose tongue is a sharp sword, then the Jews are not to blame for the death of Christ, for they were careful to keep their hands off him."[1] The whole situation was further complicated by the additional murder, under rather similar circumstances, of Archibald, Sub-Dean of Orleans. "Alas now, in the words of the prophet, 'bloodshed never ends, but it begins again' and cries out to you with a strong voice from France,"[2] wrote Bernard at this further outrage. But in spite of all Bernard's energy the whole affair seems to have been unsatisfactorily handled and Notier got off with a light sentence from a council convoked at Jouarre to deal with the matter. However the Pope, himself unsatisfied with the verdict of the council, in response to an appeal from Peter the Venerable, deprived Notier and his accomplices of all their benefices and laid under an interdict any place where they might seek refuge until such time as they had done suitable penance for their crime.

It was now time for Bernard to turn his attention again to the Count of Poitiers for, so long as he remained under the influence of Gerard, the situation in France could never be satisfactory or safe. This time he set out to interview the count, in the company of Geoffrey of Chartres, the Apostolic Legate, at Parthenay where he had a château, but the matter went badly from the start. At first the count would not see them at all, and when at last better counsels prevailed and he consented to give them a hearing, he was truculent and unfriendly. He went so far as to agree to acknowledge Innocent but, with all the obstinacy of a feeble character trying to save his self-esteem in the face of obvious defeat, he utterly refused to reinstate the bishops he had expelled from their sees. At last Bernard, his patience exhausted, brought the audience to a close by getting up and remarking as he left the chamber that he would be saying Mass for the count the next day in the church of Notre-Dame-de-la-

[1] Ep. 164 (Migne 158).
[2] Ep. 161 (Migne 155).

Couldre which adjoined the château. The following morning the church was packed to the doors, for everyone expected something to happen and there was an atmosphere of expectancy abroad. Even the count felt compelled to come although as an excommunicated person he had to remain in the porch outside the church. Everything went as usual until the kiss of peace when Bernard, holding the sacred Host in his hands, suddenly turned round and began slowly to advance down the church towards where the count stood at the door. Then confronting the count with the Host and his eyes blazing he cried: "We have petitioned you and you have ignored us; we have sat at your feet in council, and you have disdained us. Now behold the Virgin's son, the head of the Church you persecute; behold your judge before whom the heavens bow down. Do you despise him? Are you going to treat him in the same way that you treat his servants?" As the echoes of his voice died away in the vaulting a great silence fell like a cloak on the assembled congregation. The count went white and rigid, his face working and his body writhing; then he fell on the ground foaming. His servants rushed to lift him up but he fell again. Then Bernard approached and pushing him with his foot commanded him to get up: "The Bishop of Poitiers whom you expelled from his see is here," he said, "go and make your peace with him and then do penance for all your crimes." Slowly the wretched man struggled to his feet and staggered towards the bishop to give him the kiss of peace. After this he was a changed character; within a year he had founded in his territory two daughter houses of Clairvaux, and two years later he died a holy death while on pilgrimage to the shrine of St. James at Compostella. Thus Bernard stamped out the schism in its last stronghold in France.

CHAPTER XIII

THERE seems no doubt that Bernard, by his mere presence, was able to shame men into reasonable behaviour and bring the best out of them, but as soon as his back was turned their passions flamed up again. He had hardly been back in France more than a few months before Innocent was driven out of Rome and Roger began to make trouble by trying to subvert the allies. "Preserve peace with your brothers of Pisa," he wrote to the Genoese, "faith with the lord Pope, loyalty to the King, and honour amongst yourselves . . . I have heard that you have received messengers from Count Roger of Sicily, but I do not know what they brought with them or with what they returned. To tell the truth, in the words of the poet, 'I fear the Greeks when they come with gifts'. If you should discover anyone amongst you who has been so depraved as to hold out his hand for filthy lucre, take prompt cognizance of the matter and judge him as an enemy of your good name and a traitor, as one who has not scrupled to barter the good name of the commune. . . . If you must go to war, if you wish to prove your valour by contest of arms, do not fight your neighbours and friends. It were better to work off your warlike spirit by subduing the enemies of the Church and defending your honour against the Sicilians. From them your booty would be more honourably gained and more justly held. . . ."[1] The last sentence is typical of Bernard. He could understand men wishing "to prove their valour by contest of arms" although he did not approve of it, and if they must do it then for heaven's sake let them fight the enemies of the Church. But not even Bernard could ward off Roger with letters alone, and eventually the situation got so serious that Innocent was obliged to ask him to try to arrange a truce or peace between Lothair and his Hohenstaffen rivals, Conrad and Frederick, so that the Emperor might be left free to leave Germany and come to his assistance.

Bernard obeyed the Pope without delay and early in the year 1135 was on the road to Germany, but it must have been a grievous wrench for him to tear himself away from Clairvaux and the quiet round of monastic life. "Your own experience can tell you how

[1] Ep. 131 (Migne 129).

much I am suffering," he wrote to his monks from Italy. "If my absence is irksome to you, you can be sure it is more so to me. You are suffering from the absence of one person, but I am suffering from the absence of each and all of you. It is not only that I am obliged for the time being to live away from you that grieves me but I suffer also from being obliged to move in affairs that trouble the peace of my soul, and are not perhaps very compatible with my calling."[1] But his mission to Germany seems to have been a success for, towards the end of February or the beginning of March, Lothair received the surrender of both Conrad and Frederick at the Diet of Bamberg.

Trouble now broke out in France. Innocent had convoked a council to meet at Pisa on 8th May and the King, Louis the Fat, on the pretext that it would be too hot but more probably because the Pope had in some way injured his *amour propre*, took it into his head to forbid the French bishops to attend. "We are not made of ice!" Bernard wrote to him angrily, "and I, the least of your subjects in dignity although not in loyalty, tell you that it is not desirable for you to try and hinder such a great and necessary good as this council will be."[2] After this the King relented.

On his way out to Pisa Bernard was met by delegates from Milan imploring him to visit them. The Archbishop, Anselm of Puterla, who had supported both the anti-Pope and the Hohenstaffen, had been driven out and the city was in a turmoil. Bernard had no time, it was important for him to be at Pisa without delay, but he promised to visit the city on his way back.

When he arrived at Pisa everyone was glad to welcome him, and his word was listened to with respect, but the council does not appear to have been a success. The attendance was poor and nothing much seems to have been achieved, except another excommunication of the anti-Pope and his followers, but this had been tried before. Towards the close of the meeting the Bishop of Alba, who had been administering the diocese of Milan pending the election of someone to take the place of Anselm, appeared before the assembled fathers and implored the Pope to confirm the deposition of the former Archbishop and send Bernard to restore order in the city. Innocent was perfectly agreeable but decided that Bernard had better have the support of Geoffrey of Chartres, his well-tried

[1] Ep. 144 (Migne 143).
[2] Ep. 133 (Migne 255).

friend who had stood by him during that stormy interview with the Count of Poitiers and the Cardinals Guy of Pisa and Matthew of Albano, for there was the danger that the deposition of the Archbishop might make his adherents desperate and lead to further trouble.

As they were approaching crowds poured out to meet them and they were led in triumph into the city. Bernard was the chief attraction; men and women of every class and condition of life pressed around him. Some fell on the ground before him to kiss his feet, others cut pieces off his habit for the cure of their sick, and it was deemed a great thing for anyone to hear his voice or even see him. As soon as he began to broach the matter in hand the people cried out that they were willing to abide by anything he decided, and at Mass the next day he was able to administer to all the city the oath of loyalty to Innocent and Lothair, having undertaken on his side to see that there would be no reprisals and that the city would be treated leniently. In a letter written soon afterwards he described to the Empress what he had done: "When I reconciled the Milanese I did not forget your instructions. They were not received back into the favour of the lord Pope and the unity of the Church until they had openly denied Conrad, received our lord Lothair as their master and king, and with all the world acknowledged him as the august Emperor of Rome; until with hands on the Gospels they had promised, according to the wish and command of the lord Pope, that they would make full satisfaction for the injuries they have inflicted in the past; and I beg that when the time comes for them to seek through the lord Pope, as their mediator in this matter, to be received into your favour, they may experience that leniency which I myself know so well, so that they may never regret having followed good advice and may render you due service and honour. It would not do for the faithful servants who have laboured so hard in your interests to be put to shame . . ."[1]

When he had restored peace and order Bernard turned his attention to the gorgeous churches of the city and induced the people to strip them of their rich ornaments. It is difficult to understand his purpose in this for, in his Apologia, he expressly recognizes the need of decoration in secular churches; it was only for monks that he believed it inappropriate. But it is significant that he had apparently no difficulty in persuading the people to comply with his wishes in the matter. He is also recorded as having done many

[1] Ep. 139 (Migne 137).

miracles during his stay there and, perhaps the greatest of them all, he opened at Chiaravalle, in the neighbourhood, a daughter house of Clairvaux to shine as a perpetual reminder of his visit and to be a living source of spiritual strength.

In the following October trouble broke out again in Milan. The people, jealous of their supposed prerogatives, refused to allow their new Archbishop to take the customary oath of fidelity to the Pope. The poor man was in a dilemma: either he must take the oath and lose his people or refuse the oath and lose his see. As soon as Bernard heard of this new situation he wrote to Innocent, from whom he seems to have heard the news, "by intemperate action you could soon lose all that you have accomplished with these people of Milan at the cost of so much labour on the part of yourself and your servants. What is that poor bishop to do? He would like to obey you, but the beasts of Ephesus bare their teeth at him. Very prudently he is trying to disguise his sentiments for the time being, but only to incur thereby the very much more fearful wrath of yourself. . . . Can you doubt his loyalty? If any evil-minded person has tried to suggest to you the contrary, he only proves his own disloyalty by spitefully persecuting a man of such excellent character. I implore you, most loving father, to have consideration for this most loyal servant of yours . . . and I beg you to spare the people who have only just attached themselves to you."[1] And to the Milanese: "I offer you good advice: do not try too far the forbearance of the Roman Church or you will feel her power. . . . If you show the reverence that is due to her, it will be reverence without reserve, for the Apostolic See, by a unique privilege, is endowed with full authority over all the Churches of the world. Anyone who withstands this authority sets his face against the decrees of God. She can, if she judge it expedient, set up new bishops where, hitherto, there have been none. Of those which exist she can put down some and raise up others just as she thinks best. She can summon churchmen, no matter how high and mighty they may be, from the ends of the earth and bring them to her presence, not once or twice, but as often as she sees fit. Furthermore she is quick to punish disobedience if anyone should try to oppose her wishes."[2]

Having in a matter of some ten months restored order and peace to Germany and the north of Italy Bernard returned to Clairvaux

[1] Ep. 137 (Migne 314).
[2] Ep. 140 (Migne 131).

in time to keep the feast of Christmas with his monks. As soon as he had arrived his Prior, Geoffrey de la Roche, met him with the news that things could not go on as they were. They must either build a new monastery or else they must turn away the men that were coming almost every day to seek admission. It was useless to think of building on the present site, the position would not permit of it. Far better and, in the long run, more economical, to build a new monastery a little further up the valley towards the east where the river Aube could be more easily harnessed to work the mills and irrigate the land, where communications would be easier, and where the vine could be cultivated to greater advantage. This matter had been raised before and Bernard had always refused to consider it, not because he disapproved of the scheme on moral grounds but simply because he did not see how the expense could be met. But now circumstances, as Geoffrey pointed out, were different. Count Theobald was ready to defray at least the greater part of the cost and also supply the material, and in any case it was unthinkable to turn away recruits just because they had not the faith to build a larger monastery. Compelled by these arguments Bernard gave his consent and by the following Spring the building was under way. A charming story is told how the vine came to be grown at Clairvaux and wine to be made. One day the Prior found a certain lay-brother named Christian tending a vine he had been given. On his asking, rather angry and shocked, what he wanted a vine for, Brother Christian replied that he was a sinner and wanted to drink wine. The Prior reported the matter to Bernard and Bernard, so far from being shocked, took the lay-brother's side. And so the monks of Clairvaux began to drink a little wine "for their stomach's sake" and to market it, no doubt greatly to the benefit of both their health and their finances. Now Bernard was able to settle down calmly to his commentary on the Song of Songs, all the troubles and worries of the last year forgotten in the beauty of his theme and in the joy of being home again amongst his monks.

With Bernard back at Clairvaux the cause of the Pope in Italy began to stagnate; the drive had gone out of it. All the West was on his side, but the anti-Pope was firmly entrenched in Rome and the irrepressible Roger of Sicily had captured Salerno, Naples, and Capua; it looked as if he would over-run the whole peninsula, there was little enough to stop him. Men waited patiently for the promised help of the Emperor, but the days passed and it did not come. At last Innocent sent to beg him not to delay any longer and, at the same time, messengers to Clairvaux commanding the presence of Bernard. We can imagine Bernard's dismay at being called away again from Clairvaux; after barely a year's respite he must set out once more on the long and weary journey to Italy and be sucked again into the vortex of secular affairs.

Bernard had not been in Italy very long before the news came that the Emperor, accompanied by Henry the Proud, Duke of Bavaria, had crossed the Brenner pass at the head of a large army and was sweeping down through the peninsula. Soon all Italy, with the exception of Rome, had fallen to his arms. Lothair seems to have been a treacherous and truculent man more interested in extending the Empire than the welfare of the Church. During the whole campaign Bernard was occupied in trying to keep the truce between him and Innocent; there was trouble over Apulia and there was trouble over Monte Cassino; Lothair claiming them for the Empire and Innocent for the papacy. There was also trouble between Lothair and the Italian allies, and Bernard had to write him a very stern letter on his treatment of the devoted Pisans. "I wonder," he wrote, "at whose instigation you have allowed yourself to be so hoodwinked that a people who have, beyond any doubt, deserved of you a double honour, should have been treated quite to the contrary. I refer to the Pisans who were the first and, at one time, the only people to stand out in defence of the Empire."[1] Then suddenly Lothair fell ill and decided that he would return to Germany. This gave Roger just the opportunity he was looking for; he had been driven back but not defeated and with the Emperor away there was nothing to stop him ravaging the south of Italy again and, perhaps, over-running the whole country.

Once more all eyes turned to Bernard. He must go and beard the Sicilian tyrant in his den; it was the only hope. And so with a heavy heart, weary in mind and body, he dragged himself all the way back to Apulia. "My soul is sorrowful and will not be comforted until I return to you," he wrote to his monks at Clairvaux. "What consolation can there be for me in this evil hour, in this land of my exile? Wherever I am your dear memory is with me, but for this very reason your absence is all the more hard to endure. Unhappy am I to be doomed to an exile ever prolonged. . . . Sorrowfully and reluctantly, weak and sickly, and (I admit) ever haunted by the wan

[1] Ep. 143 (Migne 140).

spectre of death, I have bowed before the urgent request of the
Emperor, the command of the Apostolic See, the prayers of the
Church and of secular princes, and suffered myself to be dragged
back to Apulia."[1] What that long journey in the heats of an Italian
summer must have cost him in mere physical fatigue, quite apart
from the mental strain, cannot be imagined; the wonder is that he
survived. Even today with all the comforts of modern travel it is
no light matter for a sick man to travel in the summer from the
north of Italy down to the south.

Bernard found Roger at Salerno with all his army ready to attack
the small force of Ranulph of Alife, and the result seemed a fore-
gone conclusion; no wonder then that he refused to listen to
Bernard's suggestions of peace and merely laughed at his warning
that if he took the field he would be defeated; yet, against all human
probability, this is exactly what happened. The next day Roger
took to the field and Bernard to his prayers, and before long Roger
was flying back to Salerno for his life, his army utterly routed.
Rather sobered by this defeat he then suggested to Bernard that
there should be a public disputation between the two parties to the
schism so that he could judge on which side the right lay. The discussion took place in December with Bernard and the Cardinals
Haimeric, Gerard and Guy speaking for Innocent and the Cardinals
Matthew, Gregory and Peter of Pisa for Anacletus. The side of the
anti-Pope had the first say, and Bernard concluded on behalf of
Innocent. When his time came to speak he turned his attention to
Peter of Pisa, the only upright and wholly sincere cardinal to support Anacletus, and said: "I know you are a wise and learned man,
Peter, and I only wish that your talents were better employed in the
service of the more sound and honourable side. As for me, I am
only a countryman, more used to pushing the plough than arguing
with scholars, and were the faith not at stake I would far sooner keep
silence. But charity forces me to speak because the tunic of the Lord
which even the Jews and Romans did not dare to tear has been rent
to shreds by this man Peter Leon. There is one Lord, one baptism,
and one faith; we know nothing of two Lords, a double baptism, or
two faiths. Everyone agrees that the ark which Noe built at the
time of the flood to save the lives of eight people is a type of the
Church. Lately another ark has been built and of these two arks one
must be fraudulent and destined to sink. If the ark of which Peter

[1] Ep. 146 (Migne 144).

Leon is captain is the true ark of God, then it follows that the ark of Innocent is doomed and with it the whole Church, all the people of France, Germany, Spain, and England; all the monks of Camaldoli, the Chartreuse, Grandmont, Cluny and Citeaux and the canons of Premontré together with countless other religious Orders of men and women; all these are sitting and, as it were with mill stones round their necks, doomed to be swallowed up in the depths. Can we believe that Count Roger here of all the princes of the earth is the only one who will be saved, all the others being in the ark of Innocent? God forbid that the world should perish so that Peter Leon, with whose life and manners we are all too familiar, should alone be saved."[1] Towards the end of this discourse Peter of Pisa rose slowly to his feet and came over to Bernard who clasped him by the hand with the words, "Welcome, Peter, to the safer ark." All those present were profoundly moved with the exception of Roger who declared that the matter was beyond him and that he could not understand it. But the side of the anti-Pope was slowly crumbling, the end was in sight at last. It came more suddenly than might have been expected. In the following year on 25th January, 1138, death brought the turbulent career of Anacletus to an end. Gregory, cardinal priest of the Holy Apostles, was elected to take his place, but no one had any faith in him; by twos and threes Bernard won over his supporters, and finally on 29th May Gregory himself under cover of darkness came to Bernard and surrendered himself into his hands, so that at last he could write to his Prior at Clairvaux: "On the very octave day of Pentecost God fulfilled our desires by giving unity to the Church and peace to the city of Rome. On that day all the supporters of Peter Leon prostrated themselves at the feet of the lord Pope to take the oath of fealty and become his liege men. At last the peace has come which I felt sure would come, although I could not say when. Now nothing remains to keep me here any longer, and I can change 'I will come' for 'I am coming', as you have been imploring me to do. 'I am coming soon carrying with me my award,' the victory of Christ and the peace of the Church. And so 'I shall come back rejoicing, carrying with me the sheaves of peace'. These are fine words, but the facts are even finer, so fine that whoever is not glad must be either a fool or a knave."[2]

[1] De Vita S. Bernardi Abb. auctore Ernaldo. c. vii.
[2] Ep. 148 (Migne 317).

CHAPTER XIV

THE weary eight years of schism were over and, thanks largely to Bernard, the Church was once more united under one Pope. In the service of peace and unity Bernard had travelled France, Germany, and Italy confirming the doubtful, appeasing the quarrelsome, and stirring the apathetic. He had stood up to the Emperor and brought him to order, he had won over the King of England, he had faced the Count of Poitiers and brought him to submission, he had composed quarrels between the allies, and he had put Count Roger of Sicily to shame; if any man were entitled to a little peace and rest, to the blessing promised to peacemakers, it was he, but neither peace nor rest was to be his. The dream of resting in the cloistered peace of Clairvaux which had sustained him amidst his labours, during his interminable journeys in the noise and dust and heat up and down Italy, was to come to nothing; not for him the untroubled life of prayer and work amongst his monks for which he had sighed all these years; such hopes did not survive his journey home for, while crossing the Alps, he was met by news that robbed them of all substance. "When at last it pleased your Serenity," he wrote to the Pope from his sick bed, "to permit me to return to my brethren after the many disappointments and toils I had endured in the service of the Roman Church, I came back to my monastery broken by my labours yet nevertheless rejoicing for the peace I was able to bring with me. I believed that I had left all my troubles behind me and come at last to peace, I had hoped that I might be permitted to repair the hurt I had suffered in my spiritual life while outside the monastery; but sorrow has found me out. Now I lie prostrate on my bed, suffering more in mind than in body...."[1] Like Tithonus denied escape from misery in death by his immortality, Bernard was denied the quiet sanctuary of the cloister by his gifts and abounding charity.

What had happened was this: While Bernard was still in Rome, after the schism but before he had returned home, he was approached by the Archbishop of Lyons and two members of the Chapter of

[1] Ep. 181 (Migne 166).

Langres, to enlist his help in choosing a suitable candidate to fill the
vacancy caused by the recent death of the Bishop of Langres, the
Pope having insisted that they should be guided by the advice of
"religious persons". Bernard was a little dubious, and only after he
had been assured by the Archbishop in person that no step would be
taken without his advice did he consent to do anything in the
matter. Finally after much discussion together they chose two
candidates out of a great number and agreed that only these two
and no others should be submitted for election. The Pope then
gave his consent for the election to proceed but only on the express
condition that either one or other of the two candidates chosen in
consultation with Bernard should be adopted.

As Bernard was crossing the Alps on his way home he was met
by "certain religious persons" with the news that the Archbishop, as
soon as he had got back, had broken the agreement made in Rome
and chosen a completely different man, in fact a monk of Cluny,
as the candidate for the see of Langres. "These religious persons,"
Bernard wrote to the Pope, "were for my turning aside and passing
through Lyons so as to prevent, if I could, such a disaster from taking
place. I had intended to return the shortest way for I was tired and
ill and I did not put much trust in the rumours that had reached me.
For who could believe that such a man as the Archbishop of Lyons
would be so fickle as to disregard not only his recent promise to me
but also the mandate of his lord the Pope, and lay hands without
misgiving on a man of such evil report?"[1]

When he arrived in Lyons Bernard found the news he had heard
was indeed true and the Archbishop admitted it but laid the blame
on Odo, the son of Hugh II Duke of Burgundy, adding that,
whatever he might have done in the past, he would in future do
what Bernard wished. "Not what I wish but what God wishes,"
Bernard replied, and then said that the best way of finding what God
wished in the matter would be to submit it to a council of bishops,
and this the Archbishop seemed ready to do. Then the candidate in
question arrived in Lyons, but instead of coming to the Archbishop's
palace he put up at an inn near by and left the next day. "It is not
for me to say why he did not present himself at the curia," wrote
Bernard, "when he had come such a distance for this purpose.
It might have been on account of monastic modesty and contempt
for honours if what happened afterwards did not indicate the

[1] Ep. 179 (Migne 164).

contrary,"[1] for, although he did not come to the palace, he had it conveyed to the Archbishop that he would not accept Bernard's suggestion of submitting the matter to a council of Bishops.

Soon after this the man was invested by the King with the temporalities of the see and duly consecrated Bishop of Langres. On hearing this grievous news Bernard wrote again to the Pope saying: "Most loving father, did you not strictly command that a religious and suitable person should be chosen to fill the vacancy at Langres, and that the advice of myself, your child, should be followed in the matter? And did not my lord of Lyons receive from your Holiness in person these instructions? And did he not promise to observe them? What then does he mean by wanting to change what had been so wisely decreed, by trying on his own initiative to do something quite different and most unbecoming, so as to bring your Majesty into contempt and my own insignificant person into ridicule? Enquire, my father, enquire very carefully into the reference of that man on whom he is hastening to lay hands. Very shame forbids me to repeat what common report says of him, what his evil reputation declares of him. I did intend to write the whole sorry story from the beginning, but my hand is paralysed with sorrow, my mind is clouded with grief, and my tongue refuses to tell the evil fraud, the deceit, the villainy, the trickery, and the audacity that has been perpetrated."[2]

Whether or not Bernard's hand was really "paralysed with grief"—this was by no means the last letter he wrote on the affair—there is no doubt at all that he felt very strongly about it. At first sight it might seem strange that ill and weary as he was he did not content himself with leading a peaceful monastic life and leave the matter to take its course. He had laboured manfully in the cause of peace during the schism and might be said to have saved the Church; surely this was enough for anyone; in comparison with this a mere local squabble over the candidate for a minor see could not have seemed very important. To think like this is to misunderstand Bernard; in this squabble over the Langres election the same principles were at stake, although on a minor scale, that he had fought for during the schism and that he would fight for all his life; and, furthermore, he was intimately involved in the affair not only

[1] Ep. 179 (Migne 164).
[2] Ep. 182 (Migne 167).

because his advice had been sought in the beginning but also because Clairvaux was situated in the diocese of Langres and he would be under obedience to the bishop. It would be excessively cynical to say that his concern in the matter arose from reluctance to acknowledge as his bishop a monk of Cluny. Whether or not the man's character was as bad as Bernard implies (Peter the Venerable attributed Bernard's attitude to mere Cistercian prejudice), there is no doubt at all that the Archbishop of Lyons had acted in a high-handed not to say unscrupulous manner and that Bernard's position even from a merely canonical point of view was impregnable.

At last, after numberless tear-stained letters, Bernard won his case or, as he would say and say with truth, justice triumphed; the Pope annulled the election and instructed the Chapter of Langres to choose someone else. But this was not the end, for the Chapter immediately elected Bernard himself and, after Bernard had refused, his prior and right-hand man Geoffrey de la Roche. "The support of my weakness has been taken from me, the light of my eyes has been snatched away, my right hand has been cut off,"[1] Bernard wrote of this latest development, but after what had happened he could not very well object.

It says a great deal for both men that in spite of the rivalry between their two Orders, and "the storm of Langres", the friendship between Peter the Venerable and Bernard remained unimpaired. "I welcomed your letter with both hands. I have read it and re-read it greedily and gladly and the more often I read it the better pleased I am. I must say I enjoy your humour,"[2] Bernard wrote to him soon after the trouble over Langres, and on another occasion, when Peter had described him "as the great and glorious pillar of the whole monastic Order and indeed of the whole Church", Bernard wrote back; "O you good man, what have you done? You have praised a sinner, you have numbered a good-for-nothing amongst the blessed! You must now pray hard that I am not led into a false estimation of myself by believing what you have said."[3] And there is one charming letter in which Bernard says, "My son Nicolas, who is your son too. . . ." This is the Nicolas who afterwards disgraced himself—"is himself upset and has upset me by telling me that he noticed that one of my letters to you concluded on a

[1] Ep. 186 (Migne 170).
[2] Ep. 305 (Migne 228).
[3] Ep. 306 (Migne 265).

rather bitter note. Believe me who love you that nothing could have come from my heart or left my lips which would have offended your ears. My many occupations are to blame, because when my secretaries have not fully grasped my meaning they are apt to write too sharply, and I do not have time to read through what they have written."[1] Peter replied that he was not in the least offended by the bitter words of Bernard and that if he had been Bernard's apology made more than ample amends.

Hardly had the storm over Langres subsided than another broke out over Rheims and once again Bernard was called upon to intervene. After the death of their Archbishop, Raynald, in 1138, and during the interregnum before his successor was elected, the people of Rheims secured from the King, Louis le Jeune, authority to establish in the city a commune with a mayor at the head of it. Laon, not far away, had already obtained a similar privilege, but with one difference: at Laon the matter had been arranged with the co-operation of the bishop, at Rheims while the see was still vacant. As soon as they had obtained their charter the newly created Mayor and Aldermen immediately claimed civil and criminal jurisdiction in the city on the pretext that it had originally belonged to the people and had been usurped by the archbishops. This led to endless troubles. The Chapter appealed to the King, the King commanded the commune to respect the ancient rights of the Church, the commune ignored the command of the King, then fighting broke out and blood was shed. Bernard appealed to the Pope: "The Church of Rheims has fallen into ruin," he wrote, "the glorious city has been brought into contempt. She cries out to those who pass by that there is no sorrow like unto her sorrow. Without there is fighting and within there is fear. But there is also fighting within, for her sons are fighting against her."[2] After further delays the King commanded that the civil and criminal jurisdiction should be restored to the Church; and Geoffrey, Bishop of Chartres, and the Bishops of Soissons, Arras, and Auxerre were delegated by the Pope to arrange for the election of a new archbishop. The choice of the Chapter was unanimous: Bernard must be their archbishop, he alone could control the commune, and the King supported their choice with a letter asking him to accept: "I am very glad you are so sincere in all that appertains to the glory of God," answered

[1] Ep. 308 (Migne 387).
[2] Ep. 209 (Migne 318).

Bernard. "For, to mention nothing else, you would surely not be so very anxious to promote such a wretched person as myself except for the glory of God. You are not satisfied with simply consenting to my election, you have also added your request that I should accept it. You show me favour, you open wide your kind heart and, so that I should not be scared of the burden, you promise me the help of your royal protection. But I am a timorous character, broken in body, and there only remains for me the grave. I cannot on any account 'stretch forth my hands to great works'; unfitted and unequal to such a holy office, I cannot possibly venture to accept it. Those responsible for my election should have considered this. If they are able to overlook my insufficiency, I cannot do so; or, if they believe me suitable because of the religious habit I wear, they must understand that the habit gives the appearance of holiness, but not the virtue."[1]

While Bernard was trying to maintain the honour and integrity of the Church in France a great change was taking place in Rome or, more precisely, in the attitude and character of the Pope. The man who in adversity had been gentle and forbearing, now that he was undisputed master of Rome and Vicar of Christ, started to shed any Christ-like virtues he may have had. He hardened in his attitude towards both his former adversaries and his old friends, a note of pomposity began to creep into his rescripts and personal relations and a spirit of bitter resentment to appear against those who ventured to differ from him or who had at any time opposed him. Finally at the Lateran Council in April 1139, to the utter dismay of everyone present, he deprived all those who had ever opposed him of their insignia and offices, denouncing each of them by name, and amongst those publicly humiliated was Peter of Pisa. The news came as a bitter shock to Bernard. He had been silently watching with anxiety and sorrow the growth of this spirit of resentment and reprisal in the Pope and his entourage, but the betrayal of Peter was more than he could endure. We have already seen what sort of man Peter was; a man of great piety and distinguished learning, his doubts about the validity of Innocent's election had been sincere and his good faith unquestioned even by his adversaries. Then, before the end of the schism, when everything still hung in the balance, he had been converted by Bernard, reconciled to Innocent and, with Innocent's full authority, reinstated in all his honours.

[1] Ep. 210 (Migne 449).

Such was his moral prestige that his conversion to Innocent delivered the death blow to the party of the anti-Pope; after Peter had left him no one could believe in the validity of Anacletus's claims. And now, Innocent, having welcomed him with every show of friendship, had turned upon him. In despair Bernard took up his pen and wrote a letter in his defence, which lost him forever the Pope's friendship: "Who shall judge between us?" he wrote. "If I had a judge before whom I could summon you, I would show you (I speak as one in travail) what you deserve. . . . I arraign you against yourself, to judge between yourself and myself. What, I ask you, have I, your son, done to deserve so ill of you that you must brand and blazon me with the name and stigma of a traitor? Were you not pleased to appoint me as your representative for the reconciliation of Peter of Pisa, should God deign through me to call him from the foul condition of schism? If you deny this, I can prove it by as many witnesses as there were men in the curia at the time. And after this was not the man received back to his position and honours according to your plighted word? Who is it then who has advised you to go back on your word and to revoke what you had once granted? . . . The punishment ought to fit the crime, it ought not to be the same for a small sin as for a great one, nor is it right that he who forsook the schism should fall under the same sentence as those whom the schism forsook. For the sake of him who, that he might spare sinners, did not spare himself, remove this reproach against me and, by re-installing him whom you have once installed, honour your first wise and unbiased decision. I have written to you on this matter before, but because I never received an answer I suppose my letter did not reach you."[1] It need hardly be said that this letter also remained unanswered and Peter had to wait until the next pontificate before being re-installed. Clearly Innocent was one of those whose character is corrupted by power or who, in the common phrase, cannot carry corn. The unfortunate effects of great place on small men are a subject not unworthy of attention nor wholly irrelevant to our own times.

Meanwhile trouble was coming to meet Bernard from another quarter and from a very different and, in many ways, far greater man than Pope Innocent. For some time now Bernard had been viewing with disfavour the novel theological opinions of a brilliant

[1] Ep. 283 (Migne 213).

young man called Peter Abelard and during the Spring of 1141 he heard from the Archbishop of Sens that Abelard had challenged him to a public disputation in defence of his opinions on the first Sunday after Pentecost.

CHAPTER XV

THE most superficial acquaintance with Bernard's writings should be enough to convince anyone that he was a scholar of the highest order, and the contents of the library at Clairvaux in his day proves that he was no opponent of monastic studies.[1] Not only a scholar but also a patron of scholars, Bernard advised our own Robert Pullen, to whom Oxford University owes so much, to study at Paris and got himself into very hot water with the Bishop of Rochester for his pains: "I have not deserved your severe letter. I advised Robert Pullen to spend some time at Paris for the sake of the sound learning to be found there because I thought it necessary for him, and I still do,"[2] he wrote in reply to an angry letter from the bishop. Nevertheless Bernard was not in favour of learning just for the sake of learning; he held very strongly that knowledge should be fruitful in charity, and a quest for truth that never led to the contemplation of truth seemed to him rather futile. When he said that the purpose of studies was our own edification and the edification of our neighbour[3] he did not mean that we should confine our reading to little books of devotion; his age was happily rather poorer than ours in this type of literature if such it can be called, and, as we have seen, he took for granted a love of Ovid in one of his monks, but he did mean that our study of theology should lead us to union with God and should have some effect on our lives; otherwise, so he thought, it is apt to end in mere vanity.

No wonder, therefore, that with these views Bernard found himself but little in sympathy with Peter Abelard, nor indeed was he alone in his antipathy to the teaching of this dour young man. Abelard's career had been stormy; destined for the military life by

[1] "The library at Clairvaux was initiated by St. Bernard, who had no predilection for a cult of either ugliness or stupidity. Most of the works of the Fathers and of the writers of the Carolingian renaissance found a place in the library. . . . It is evident therefore that St. Bernard had very different views from De Rance in the matter of studies." *Citeaux and Her Elder Daughters* by Archdale King, p. 219. Burns & Oates, 1954.

[2] Ep. 271 (Migne 205).

[3] Serm. in Cant. xxxvi. 3.

his father he quickly abandoned it in favour of learning, and very soon began to blaze through the old-fashioned schools of his day offending all his masters, putting them out of countenance and sometimes out of court by his precocious brilliance. Otto of Freising, a contemporary who sat under him for a time, tells us that he was so arrogant and self-opinionated that he could scarcely demean himself to listen to his masters, and he certainly has not one kind or generous word to say of them; yet these men, William of Champeaux and Anselm of Laon, were no dullards, old-fashioned and stuffy perhaps, but neither ignorant nor foolish. When the schools of Paris at last closed their doors to him, nothing daunted he outraged the etiquette of the time by opening a school of his own at Ste. Geneviève, just outside Paris, but such was the brilliance and novelty of his teaching that it was not long before students were leaving their old masters to sit at his feet. Then he broke away and fled to Brittany where he secretly married Héloise, and when, owing to the rather drastic intervention of the bride's uncle, the marriage could not go according to plan, he became a monk of St. Denis at Paris and she a nun at the Abbey of Argenteuil. He did not stay long at St. Denis; the monks, enraged by his criticism of their lives and even more by the aspersions he cast on the legend of their patron Saint, got rid of him as soon as they could. They parted amid mutual recriminations. Soon afterwards his book on the Trinity was condemned and he fled to a remote spot near Nogent-sur-Seine where he built a hermitage which he dedicated to the Paraclete and lived for a time with one companion, but his fame spread and disciples came to him even here. Not long after this he seems to have been elected abbot of St. Gildas de Rhuys, a house of Black Monks in Brittany; but here again he did not settle: "I fell," he said, "into hands of Christian monks wilder and worse than pagans," and returned to his hermitage. By this time it was no longer a hermitage because Héloise had gone to live there from Argenteuil bringing some of the nuns with her. Here Abelard remained for a time ruling the community with Héloise, only to return again after a while to Paris and teaching.

There can be no question of Abelard's brilliance and there can be little doubt of his good faith, but he undoubtedly depended far too much on unenlightened human reason for understanding the mysteries of religion. "I applied myself first of all," he wrote, "to discussing the fundamental principles of our faith in the light of human reason and in my book on the Unity and Trinity of God to composing a treatise for my disciples who demanded human and philosophical reasons and demonstrations rather than affirmations. They thought it futile to speak in a manner that could not be understood since it is not possible for anyone to believe anything unless he first understand it."[1] To approach the mystery of the Trinity in this way is really too much; naturally and quite rightly Bernard, the last of the Fathers, took alarm. It was not as if Abelard was an unknown master lecturing in some remote cloister, men were flocking to him from all over Europe and his doctrine had found supporters even in Rome. "Master Abelard," wrote Bernard, "is a monk without a rule, a prelate without responsibility; he is neither in order nor of an Order. He argues about faith against the faith; he assails law against the law. He sees nothing 'through a glass in a dark manner, but views everything face to face', dwelling on high matters, on marvels beyond his reach! . . . Raw and inexperienced listeners hardly finished with their dialectics, and those who can hardly, so to speak, digest the first elements of the faith, are introduced by him to the mystery of the Holy Trinity, to the Holy of Holies, to the chamber of the King, and to him who is 'shrouded in darkness'."[2] These are hard words, but they were true and under the circumstances they were called for. How easy it is to see these young students, who are much the same in all ages and all over the world, flocking to hear this brilliant young professor making a laughing stock of all the old masters. In Bernard and Abelard two different worlds faced each other: the old world of the Fathers and the new world of scholasticism, and it was too much to expect them to agree, but by his arrogant bumptiousness Abelard spoilt what chances there may have been of agreement. No doubt much of what he said needed saying, but he went too far; mere cleverness is never enough, least of all in the great mysteries of our religion; he needed to learn his limitations, and the time was approaching when he would.

Abelard was perfectly aware of Bernard's hostility and all he longed for was, in the common phrase, "to have a go at him". The King of France and most of the bishops were to meet at Sens on the Sunday within the octave of Pentecost in the year 1140 for a solemn exposition of relics. Here Abelard saw his opportunity for

[1] His. Calam. Migne. Patrologia Latina. Tom 178.
[2] Ep. 241 (Migne 193) and Ep. 240 (Migne 192).

confronting Bernard and he jumped at it. Through the Archbishop
of Sens he challenged him to a public disputation in the presence of
the King and all the bishops of France; he had not the slightest
doubt that he would succeed in discomfiting Bernard and putting
him to shame as easily as he had his old masters in Paris. "At his
request," Bernard wrote to Pope Innocent, "the Archbishop of Sens
wrote to me fixing the day on which Abelard, in his presence and
in the presence of his brother bishops, should establish, if he could,
his perverse doctrines, against which I have dared to croak. I refused
because I am but a child in this sort of warfare and he is a man
habituated to it from his youth, and because I deemed it an unseemly
action to bring the faith into the arena of controversy, resting as it
does on sure and immutable truth. I said that his writings were
evidence enough against him, and that it was the business of the
bishops to adjudicate on the doctrines of which they were the
ministers. But he lifted up his voice all the more for this, called upon
many, and assembled all his accomplices. He spread it about on all
sides that he was going to answer me at Sens on the day appointed.
The word of it went forth to everyone, and I was not able to hide
myself. At first I did nothing, not greatly caring for what people
were saying. Yet, unwillingly and sorrowfully, I bowed to the
advice of my friends, who saw how everyone was preparing as if for
a show, and feared that my absence would serve only to increase the
influence of the man and the scandal of the people, also it seemed
that his errors might appear to be confirmed if there were no one to
answer and refute them."[1]

And so Bernard went to meet Abelard at Sens, unwillingly,
sorrowfully and, as he himself tells us, "unprepared and unprotected
except by those words which I had in mind at the time 'Take no
thought of how and what to speak: for it will be given to you in that
hour what to speak' and 'With the Lord to aid me I have no fear
of the worst that men can do'."[2] He found the whole city decked
out for a public holiday and men pointing out Abelard as he
strutted about surrounded by a crowd of admirers and disciples.
Emaciated, weak and ill at ease in all this gay concourse, Bernard
must have cut a different figure. After the veneration of the relics
Bernard preached to the people and asked them to pray for Abelard.
There was of course no harm in this, we all of us need prayers; but

[1] Ep. 239 (Migne 189).
[2] Ibid.

to commend a man in public to the prayers of the faithful does suggest that he is in a bad way and stands in special need of prayers. Abelard may have been in special need of prayers, but Bernard was not to know this for he had not yet been condemned; it was still possible that his teaching might receive the approval of the bishops.

After supper all the bishops met in council while the works of Abelard were produced and the suspected passages read out to them. The learned Watkin Williams doubts whether this preliminary meeting was either fair or canonical on the grounds that it meant that Abelard was condemned unheard, or that it was at least prejudicial to a fair hearing. It is difficult to agree with this view; the doctrines of Abelard were under judgement and they stood or fell by what he taught in his books, but it would have been impossible to judge them soberly and calmly at the public disputation without some previous knowledge of them. It was not a case of condemning him unheard, it was a case of judging what he had already taught, hearing what he had to say in defence of his teaching afterwards.

On the following day the council met formally in the Cathedral. Bernard got up and read out what he considered the objectionable passages in Abelard's works and called on him to defend them; but Abelard, who had been so brave in confuting his masters and had come to Sens so full of confidence, to everybody's amazement refused to reply to Bernard: "I will not answer the Cistercian," he said, "I appeal to Rome." To this day it remains a mystery why his courage failed at the last moment; it had never failed him before. It was not as if he were alone in a hostile crowd, he was at a meeting he had arranged himself and he was surrounded by his disciples and admirers. But instead of seizing this opportunity which he himself had arranged for justifying himself and putting Bernard to confusion, he appealed to Rome, and to Rome he would have to go. He had friends and disciples amongst the cardinals in curia and would certainly have a fair hearing there. After this there was nothing left for the assembled bishops to do but hand the matter over to Rome. They made a collection of what they considered objectionable passages from the books of Abelard and sent them off under cover of a letter signed by the Archbishop of Sens, the Apostolic Legate, and the Bishops of Orleans, Auxerre, Troyes, and Meaux. The Archbishop of Rheims and three of his suffragans who had been present at the council also wrote, and Bernard too wrote a personal letter to the Pope. "Fool that I am," he wrote, "I was but lately promising myself rest, when the madness of Peter the lion had been quelled and peace restored to the Church. And now the Church is at peace, but not I. We have escaped Peter the lion only to fall victims to Peter the dragon. The books of this man have wings . . . they pass from country to country, and from one kingdom to another. A new gospel is being forged . . . virtues and vices are being discussed immorally, the sacraments of the Church falsely, the mystery of the Trinity neither simply nor soberly. Everything is put quite differently from what we have been accustomed to hear."[1] The last sentence is important; it was not only Abelard's doctrine that was objectionable, it was his method of approach, and his lack of reverence.

Then Bernard himself published a summary of Abelard's errors and his refutation of them. This is not one of his best treatises, it lacks his usual serenity, it gives the impression that he was emotionally involved in the matter and even rather angry, yet there are some fine passages in it and one feels that after all perhaps Abelard was wise not to meet him in public discussion. One quotation must suffice; the whole of Abelard's doctrinal errors seem to stem from his having a mistaken idea of faith and this is how Bernard deals with it: "It is not surprising that this man who does not care what he says and who lays violent hands on the mysteries of our faith and who irreverently raids the hidden treasures of our piety, should speak impiously of faith itself. At the very beginning of his book on Theology, or rather Stultology, he defines faith as opinion; as if, indeed, a man were at liberty to think and talk about it as he liked! As if the sacred things of our faith depended on vague surmise and were not founded on the solid basis of certain truth. If our faith were thus unsure would not our hope also be uncertain? How foolish our martyrs would have been to suffer so much for so long for something so doubtful! How can anyone dare to describe our faith as a mere opinion unless he has not yet received the Holy Spirit or is ignorant of the Gospels or thinks them no better than fables. 'I know in whom I have believed and I am sure of him,' cries the Apostle, and does this man mutter to me that it is only a matter of opinion? Quite otherwise Saint Augustine who said, 'faith is held in the heart of the believer from him in whom he

[1] Ep. 239 (Migne 189).

believes not by conjecture or opinion, but by certain knowledge and the witness of conscience'."[1]

Abelard seems to have got no further on his way to Rome than Cluny when he was met by the news that his teaching had been condemned in Rome, his books publicly burnt, and he himself put under sentence of staying in a monastery—surely no very great hardship for one who was both a monk and an abbot! The ever charitable Peter the Venerable obtained permission for him to remain at Cluny where he became one of the community and, two years later, died a pious and holy death. It is pleasant to know that before he died he was reconciled with Bernard and able to inform Peter the Venerable that their ancient quarrels were now appeased.

Although it is nearly nine hundred years since Peter Abelard died his romantic figure still remains a centre of controversy. On the one hand his admirers greet him as a sort of Morning Star of the Reformation and Free Thought, as a brilliant and original thinker brutally suppressed and persecuted by an obscurantist monk and an ignorant body of bishops. On the other hand, there are those who denounce him as an unprincipled and unscrupulous heretic, filled with his own conceit. But, as usual, the truth seems to lie between these two extremes. There can be no doubt at all of Abelard's brilliance and charm. Even William of St. Thierry, who was the first to take alarm at his teaching and urge Bernard to combat it, writes of him: "God knows I love this man," adding with regard to his teaching, "but in a case like this no one is my friend, no one my kinsman."[2] Nevertheless his character seems to have been marred by a certain intellectual bumptiousness, by something of the precocious undergraduate, and by a hot-headed intolerance of men

[1] Tractatus de Erroribus Abelardi, c. 4.

Bernard quotes Abelard as defining faith with the word "aestimatio", but in fact "existimatio" is the word he uses: "Est quippe fides existimatio rerum non apparentium," Intro. ad Theologiam c. 1. However this does not affect the point of Bernard's argument against him as, in this context, "aestimatio" and "existimatio" are synonymous, if anything "existimatio" implies greater vagueness. But Abelard's thought on the matter seems rather confused. He wrote a crisp and elegant Latin, but a careful study of his writings does not reveal quite the clear thinker one would expect. Thus in one place he quotes with approval his disciples saying: "nec credi posse aliquid nisi prius intellectum" (Hist. Calam. P.L. t.178) and in another: "Credi salubriter debet quod explicari non valet, praesertim cum nec pro magno habendum sit, quod humana infirmitas disserere sufficit, nec pro fide reputandum, quod de manifestis recipimus humana compulsi ratione . . ." (Intro. ad Theol. ibid.).

[2] Inter Epistola S. Bernardi Ab. 236.

older and wiser than himself. Nor can there be any doubt that much of his doctrine if not blatantly heretical was at least extremely hazardous, conceivably safe in the hands of a master, but very apt to be misunderstood by enthusiastic disciples. Mistaken he certainly was, but equally certainly he was not a formal heretic. He had no intention whatever of teaching heresy, and his faults which were largely on the surface concealed a truly devout and religious spirit. Yet there can be no doubt at all that Bernard was justified in his hostility to much of Abelard's teaching; not only was it mistaken, it was very dangerously mistaken. His definition of faith as a matter of opinion is a case in point. The only question can be whether Bernard in his abhorrence of heresy and pride and his anxiety for the faith of simple people chose the best possible way of dealing with the situation. On the other hand we must remember that Abelard challenged him; left to himself it is quite probable that Bernard would not have done anything in the matter. It was not a case of Bernard harassing Abelard but of Abelard harassing Bernard.

"I do not want to be a philosopher," wrote Abelard towards the end of his life, "at the price of being rejected by Paul; nor yet an Aristotle at the price of being rejected by Christ, for there is no other name under heaven whereby I can be saved. I adore Christ reigning at the Father's right hand. With the arms of faith I embrace him working divinely in that glorious virginal flesh which he received of the Holy Ghost." It would not be a bad thing if all his modern apologists could say as much.[1]

The danger of Abelard's personal influence if not of his doctrine on the young men of his time is well illustrated by the career of the demagogue and heretic Arnald of Brescia. As his name indicates Arnald was born in Brescia, probably about the year 1094; he was educated in his home town and received there minor orders. After this he travelled in France where he fell under the influence of Abelard and remained to the end one of his most loyal and devoted supporters; Bernard tells us in a letter to the Pope that he was present at Sens: "Goliath advances tall of body, girt in the noble accoutrements of war, and preceded by his armour-bearer, Arnald of Brescia.[2] In the year 1130 he became a canon regular at Brescia, but does not seem to have remained there for long. Under Abelard's

[1] Cf. *St. Bernard of Clairvaux* by Watkin Williams. Manchester University Press, pp. 289–312.
[2] Ep. 239 (Migne 189).

influence he became a zealous reformer, very austere of life but with no consideration for the perfectly natural and reasonable limitations of those whom he made the victims of his zeal. His remedy for the ills of the time was perfectly simple, it was merely to strip the clergy of all their material wealth, and to this plan he added, for good measure, heretical views on the sacraments. It can be easily imagined how popular his plan was with the rabble who saw in it a quick and easy way to improve their lot at others' expense without the trouble of hard work; and with some of the great lords who saw in it an opportunity of at once curbing the power of the Church and satisfying their greed. Untrammelled by any respect for authority or any particular scruples, Arnald had no difficulty in stirring up trouble all over France, Italy and Germany. Bernard combated him on every front but with small success. Silenced and condemned in one place Arnald cropped up in another, no one seems to have been able to suppress him, and he lived on to trouble the pontificates of Innocent, Celestin, Lucius, and Eugenius. In Rome he roused the rabble by preaching that the Pope had no jurisdiction outside purely ecclesiastical matters. Pope Lucius lost his life through excessive zeal in leading his troops against the rioters and his successor, the Cistercian Eugenius, was unable to enter the city after his election. Bernard wrote to Conrad, the Emperor, to enlist his support in defence of the Pope: "Gird your sword upon your thigh, most powerful one," he wrote, "and let Cæsar restore to himself what is Cæsar's and to God what is God's. It is clearly the concern of Cæsar both to defend his own crown and to succour the Church,"[1] a very eloquent letter but not particularly successful; he then wrote another to the Roman People, equally eloquent and equally futile.[2] At last the Romans cut their own throats by declaring war on the more powerful people of Tivoli and Eugenius was able to enter his city with the victorious army. But, more distinguished for the holiness of his life than for any great intelligence, Eugenius seems to have been hoodwinked by the austere demeanour of Arnald and to have set him at large and absolved him on the condition that he kept silence and behaved himself in future. Arnald, who had no more respect for his promise than for the Pope, immediately returned to making trouble in Rome, by inveighing against both the cardinals and the Pope and tempting the people to rise against them by the

[1] Ep. 320 (Migne 244).
[2] Ep. 319 (Migne 243).

glittering prospect of loot. He was not finally brought to book until after the death of both Bernard and Eugenius when the English Pope Hadrian captured him and handed him over to the Emperor to be silenced for good after the fashion of the times.

CHAPTER XVI

SOME time during the year 1141 disturbing news of trouble reached Bernard from England, and he was soon involved in a controversy which became so complicated and so heated that to this day historians have not fully disentangled its threads.

It all started with the election of a successor to Thurston, the Archbishop of York, who died in February 1141, and from the very first, on the King vetoing one of the candidates, Waldef, a Cistercian of Kirkham, it was clear that difficulties would arise. After long discussion the Chapter elected their treasurer, William Fitzherbert, a nephew of the King, but the circumstances were suspicious and the Cistercian abbots of Rievaulx and Fountains began to make trouble. In virtue of the rights granted to them by the Lateran Council in 1139 they had an active interest in the election and took their responsibility seriously. It is not necessary to believe that they acted through motives of pique because one of their number had been vetoed by the King; the reputation of Fitzherbert seems to have left something to be desired and his election was open to the charges of intrusion and simony. Of course they wrote to Bernard on the matter and of course Bernard took up their defence with all the impetuous ardour of his temperament. If anyone was scandalized Bernard was on fire, but if anyone laid a finger on any of his dear sons he was on the warpath; everything they said must be true, Fitzherbert must be the most arrant rogue. In his usual manner he began to storm Pope Innocent with letters, but unfortunately none of these first letters of his on the matter have survived.

At this point Henry de Blois, Bishop of Winchester, intervened by advising Fitzherbert, in view of the trouble brewing, to take his cause to Rome. Henry was a forcible character whose ambition it was to raise Winchester to metropolitan rank with York as a mere suffragan see. As soon as the Yorkshire Cistercians heard that Fitzherbert had left for Rome they too packed off a delegation led by Ailred of Rievaulx to put their side of the story to the Pope, and Bernard wrote to the Pope: "Since many are called and few are chosen, it is no argument in favour of anything doubtful that many approve of it. The Archbishop of York is coming to see you, the same man about whom I have already written to you; he is a man who puts not his trust in God his helper but in the abundance of his riches. His case is weak and feeble and I have it on the authority of truthful men that he is rotten from the soles of his feet to the crown of his head."[1] The truthful men he refers to are undoubtedly the Yorkshire Cistercians, and as they were on the spot they should have been well informed.

On their way to Rome the Cistercian delegation stopped at Clairvaux for an interview with Bernard and then went on fortified with several introductions from him to cardinals in curia and friends in the city. To the Pope he wrote: "These men whom you see before you are true, honest and God-fearing. They have been led by the spirit of God into your august presence with the sole intention of seeking and obtaining justice. Let your eyes rest upon these weary and poor men, for not without reason have they come to you from so far, undismayed by the great distance, the dangers of the sea, the snows of the Alps and, although poor men, the expense of the journey,"[2] and to Cardinal Gerard: "The bearers of this letter, being true, honest, and God-fearing men, have undertaken the fatigues of their long journey for God's sake and not their own. It is all the more certain that they are inspired by love of justice and zeal for the house of God since it is so very evident that they do not stand to gain anything for themselves and do not hope to."[3]

The case was heard in Rome during March 1142. The evidence was strong against the archbishop-elect but broke down because the canons disallowed second-hand evidence as grounds for proceeding against anyone. The Pope sent the litigants back to England and ordered the principals to come to Rome the following year on the third Sunday in Lent.

Both parties arrived in Rome for the second hearing of the case on 7th March, 1143. As on the previous occasion the Cistercian delegation stopped at Clairvaux on the way and they brought away with them a particularly charming letter of introduction from Bernard to a lady in the city: "These abbots," he wrote, "are from our house. They are devout and thoroughly praiseworthy men.

---

[1] Ep. 187 (Migne 346).
[2] Ep. 188 (Migne 347).
[3] Ep. 189 and New Documents in the case of St. William of York by C. H. Talbot. *Cambridge Historical Journal.*

I am anxious to send you my greetings by them lest you should think I have forgotten your kindness to me when I was in the city."[1] However once again the case broke down, this time because Fitz-herbert, who seems to have been a rather adroit gentleman, appealed to the testimony of William St. Barbe, Dean of York, who was not present in Rome. The Pope sent them all home again and made his approval of the election depend on William St. Barbe swearing that pressure had not been brought to bear on the Chapter by the King. This put St. Barbe into a corner; he was too good a man to perjure himself and too timid a man to annoy the King by telling the truth. Somehow or other he managed to evade the issue by substituting someone else to take the oath in his place. It is not clear how he managed this, but he may have made his recent appointment to the see of Durham an excuse. By this time Bernard had written to Henry de Blois saying: "I advise you in all friendliness, exhort you reverently and implore you earnestly to conclude this affair in such a way that there shall be no breath of unpleasant suspicion to tarnish the credit that will be due to you."[2] So far feelings had not begun to run very high, that is to say the parties had not yet come to calling each other names. Soon Bernard would be referring to Henry de Blois as "that old whore of Winchester".[3] At about this stage he also wrote to King Stephen: "The King of Kings has for long chastised your royal Majesty, for he is more powerful than you. Yet I believe he has done it more in mercy than in anger because we know that he never forgets to be merciful even in his righteous fury. For this reason I humbly advise you and on bended knee implore you that on those matters for which above all God is especially chastising you and your realm, to wit the affairs of Church and State, you give not the Spouse of the Church further cause for punishing you yet more harshly and even completely destroying you. Especially in the case of the church of York do I implore you with my whole heart to change your attitude and not attempt to hinder the termination of the affair according to the manner laid down by the lord Pope."[4] History does not record what King Stephen thought of this letter, he was rather occupied at the time and may not have given it much attention.

[1] Ep. 194. And in original Latin in op. cit. sup.
[2] Ep. 195, op. cit.
[3] Ep. 204. Original in Hüffer.
[4] Ep. 197. Original C. H. Talbot, op. cit.

The witnesses that St. Barbe had substituted for himself had no scruples at all about taking the oath and Fitzherbert was consecrated Archbishop of York on 23rd September, 1143. Bernard, as soon as he heard the news, immediately wrote off to William, Abbot of Rievaulx, to console him and also to advise discretion. William appears to have been rather hot-headed and Bernard feared that he might make matters worse by doing something rash. After wishing him in the formula of greeting "a spirit wise and discerning, a spirit prudent and strong" he goes on to say: "I have heard what has been done about that archbishop. So I am writing to console you, for your zeal is well known to me and it would ill become our Order and not help your house if it were to flare up beyond the bounds of discretion and prudence".[1] With the decline of their cause the Cistercians began to lose courage and in order to put a little spirit into them Bernard planned to visit them himself, but the prospect of the sea voyage appears to have been too much for him and he sent instead Henry Murdac, the Abbot of Vauclair, who had one time been a monk of Clairvaux. It was doubtless a good choice, for Murdac was a Yorkshireman with influential connections in the county, but he gives the impression of being a rather dour and unsympathetic man with very little imagination. "Who will give me the wings of a dove," Bernard wrote to them, "that I may go up to this people of ours which is girded for battle, that I may behold the joy of your fraternal love, that I may share in the troubles that abound in your place of pilgrimage, that I may save those who 'perish from fears and the storms around them'. I am obliged to go out of my house on visitations by the Rule of our Order, by the duty of our fraternity, but charity spurs me on to attempt something greater than this.

"Willingly would I go and see how my brethren and their flocks are faring and bring back word to my father Jacob . . . I am the least of my brethren, but I would not fear to smite the Philistine while he upbraids the hosts of Israel with a stone from my sling . . . but the way is hard and difficult and my body is weak. On the top of this, in spite of my weakness, the journeyings I have to make on the business of the Order and in the cause of the Church 'tower high above me and hang on me like a heavy burden'. Because of this I am sending for your visitation my brother and dear friend, Henry, Abbot of Vauclair. Hear him, I beg you, as if he were myself. He

[1] Ep. 199 (Migne 353).

is an upright and sensible man who has taken on his shoulders some of my own cares and burdens. . . ."[1]

By this time Innocent had died and was succeeded by Pope Celestine II. Bernard immediately wrote to the new Pope to put him *au courant* with the state of affairs in Yorkshire. "It behoves your Holiness to raise up seed to your dead brother according to the righteousness of the law," he begins, and then goes on to explain his meaning: "This you will best do by maintaining the decrees of your predecessor Pope Innocent and completing the work he had begun. You have a case on hand now in which you can do this." He then describes in vigorous language what has happened in Yorkshire and concludes, "A man publicly infamous, accused before the Courts and not cleared, but rather condemned, has become a bishop! Let him who laid hands on him consider whether I would not do better to say he had been 'execrated' rather than 'consecrated'. Perhaps someone will say that sentence was never pronounced against this man, that he was never pronounced guilty. But I say that his action in trying to shelter behind William the dean[2] so as to avoid judgement because he could not clear himself was tantamount to a confession of guilt.

"Things being in this state you must see to it, my lord and father, that your heart does not decline unto wickedness. What advice do you propose to give to those wretched abbots who were dragged all the way to Rome as witnesses against this man? Are they to obey and receive the sacraments from one who has twice been intruded on his church, by the King and by the legate? It was the legate, who, when he could not get him through the door, dug a way for him into the sanctuary with a spade of silver, as the saying is, against the commands of the Supreme Pontiff and much to the injury of the Apostolic See and Roman Curia."[3] Pope Celestine died in 1144, before he could take any action on this letter beyond depriving Henry of Blois of his legateship, and he was succeeded by Lucius II, a friend of Bernard.

Bernard seems to have lost no time at all in acquainting Lucius with the situation both by a personal visit and by letter: "I returned home," he wrote to him, "from that excellent meeting with your curia strengthened by the grace of God and delighting in your most

[1] Ep. 201. Original C. H. Talbot, op. cit.
[2] This is William St. Barbe. There are no less than three Williams involved.
[3] Ep. 202 (Migne 235).

efficacious help. Since then I have been awaiting the hoped-for issue of the affair we settled. I have been waiting to see if the flower of the decision you made in Rome would bear appropriate fruit in Winchester so that the cup of my joy may be filled. . . . Happy Winchester, a city so powerful that it can withstand the authority of the fathers in curia, change their decrees, pervert their judgements, defame truth, and with a great voice confirm what Rome has most rightly judged shall not be confirmed without the prescribed condition of an oath! For when the dean was invited to take the prescribed oath, he not only refused to do so, but even declared himself ready to take an oath to the contrary. Yet that Philistine[1] in a spirit of turbulence does not blush to set up that idol Dagon[2] next to the very ark of the Lord. Surely he has the effrontery of the harlot spoken of by Jeremias the prophet. Winchester has arrogated to herself the venerable name of Rome, and not only the name but the prerogatives as well. . . . Lest such contumacy should become a custom and an example, lest the dignity of Rome should be torn to shreds, lest the authority of Peter succumb to these new and great humiliations, lest religion become cold in the diocese of York, yes, lest it be wholly up-rooted and scattered to the winds, let Rome in the sole interests of justice crush the contumacy of this stubborn man, and with the hammer of severity throw down the idol he has set up, and break his throne to pieces. If any of them should come to Rome for the pallium, it behoves your Holiness manfully to resist them, despising Ananias and Sapphira with their money-bags. For we fear and dread lest that old whore of Winchester should be asked in some way by the new prophet he has set up[3] to share in the government, yea in the full power of the diocese. . . ."[4] Perhaps it is needless to say that after this letter the efforts of Henry de Blois to regain the legatine authority he had lost in the previous pontificate came to nothing. Instead Hincmar, the Cardinal Bishop of Frascati, was appointed and dispatched to England with instructions to look into the matter of the York election and not to give the pallium to the Archbishop unless he was satisfied that all was in order. He paused at Clairvaux on the way, and in the following year returned to Rome without bestowing the pallium. During

---

[1] Henry de Blois.
[2] St. William of York.
[3] Again St. William of York.
[4] Ep. 204 and Hüffer.

his absence in the year 1145, Pope Lucius died and was succeeded by Eugenius III, the first Cistercian Pope.

The first action of Eugenius was to suspend Fitzherbert until William St. Barbe, now Bishop of Durham, should take the formal oath that had been required by Pope Innocent, probably because of a letter he had received from Bernard explaining the situation to him as he saw it. "I am importunate," he wrote, "but I have reason to be and my reason is the apostolate of Eugenius! For they are saying that it is not you but I who am the Pope and from all sides they are flocking to me with their suits. In such a crowd there are some whom I cannot refuse to help without scandal, even without sin. My pen is again directed against that idol of York, with all the more reason because my other attacks with this weapon have not gone home. . . ."[1] This time Bernard's attack did go home: but the suspension of Fitzherbert brought about an outbreak of violence against the Yorkshire Cistercians by the King's men, and once more Bernard wrote to the Pope: "Thwarted ambition is raging, it is indeed mad with despair. That man of perdition is careering towards his fall. That accursed tree, full not of fruit but of thorns, is anticipating the hand of the feller and provoking him to execution. How much better if he had fallen long ago rather than those good men whom by standing he has overthrown. Now they who were standing to so much better purpose than he, have fallen in their innocence and for their innocence. But their harmless blood will be required of those who by their secret support lent that poisonous tree strength to stand lest it should fall immediately. The blood of the saints calls out against them from the earth, the blood of those who are in the hand of God and beyond the reach of torment. Yet they were my children and they have been scattered. Words are no consolation, and if they were some comfort and remedy, they fail me for grief, sorrow shuts them off, my sighs interrupt them. But I have one thing to say, and it is my last, something that it is easier to write than to speak. Listen, or rather read! If this man shall survive, I very much fear that it will be for your fall, and whatever more he should do, like an evil tree that cannot give good fruit, will be held to your account and not any longer to his."[2] It is evident that Bernard felt very strongly about this affair at York, but the rumours he had heard of the violence against his sons must have been exaggerated

[1] Ep. 206 (Migne 239).
[2] Ep. 208 (Migne 251).

because there is no record of any Cistercian being killed. The affair was now drawing to a close. William St. Barbe had expressed his misgivings about the legality of the election in a letter to Cardinal Hincmar, and when he openly and frankly refused to perjure himself by taking the oath William Fitzherbert was deposed and a new election ordered. The Chapter met at Richmond on 27th July, 1147, and without much hesitation chose Henry Murdac to be their Archbishop, but it was not until the year 1151 that the clergy would accept him in the diocese, and in the meantime William had fled to Winchester and taken refuge with Henry de Blois.

In fairness to Fitzherbert it should be said that his cause did not lack the support of serious and devout men. He gives the impression of being a colourless and weak man caught up by forces he was not strong enough to control and used by stronger men than he to further their own ambitions. But there can be little doubt that the King did bring pressure to bear on the Chapter to elect him, for the Archbishop of York was a powerful temporal as well as spiritual lord and the King wanted one of his own kin to hold an office in which anyone unfavourable to him might have done much to undermine his cause in the North. However when Murdac died the Chapter once again elected him, and this time his election was un-contested and confirmed by Rome. He died some years later in the odour of sanctity and was afterwards canonized as St. William of York. His feast was kept with great solemnity in the north and a story of his life, more remarkable perhaps for edification than strict historical accuracy, embodied in the Yorkshire Breviary. "Blessed William of York," we are told, "sprang from the illustrious family of Stephen, King of England, being the son of the most puissant Count Herbert by Emma the sister of the King. Having become treasurer of the York Cathedral Chapter, he distributed all his goods to the poor believing that to earn the prayers of the poor by alms was more profitable than any material treasure. When Archbishop Thurston died the Chapter met and elected their treasurer, he blessed William who was also a treasury of merits, to succeed him. But some priests of the said church being devoured by lust for power caused dissension amongst the canons and formed a party hostile to the election. The matter was therefore referred to Rome where the election was examined and nothing found against it. But the Supreme Pontiff Eugenius, a monk of the most holy Cistercian Order, suppressed the election not because of any fault to be found in it but because he willed it so and his will was law, and with the appearance of zeal for holiness consecrated Henry Murdac, also a monk of the most holy Cistercian Order, as pastor of the church of York. In face of the poisonous tongues of his detractors the most holy servant of God had only his patience to console him, but he most wisely hastened to take refuge with Henry of Winchester where he remained for seven years. When death, who makes no distinction between rich and poor, at last brought the lives of both the Supreme Pontiff and the Archbishop of York to an end, the Blessed William set out once more for Rome where the Pope, who was his friend, regretting much the decision of his predecessor expressed himself ready to accept him as Archbishop of York on the Chapter agreeing once more to elect him."[1] After reading this it will come as no surprise to learn that St. William of York shone with miracles as well as virtues.

[1] York Breviary. Surtees Society. 1872.

CHAPTER XVII

ONE of the many endearing and human traits in the character of Bernard was that he could never see any good in his enemies or any evil in his friends and was quite incapable of undertaking anything either on their behalf or on behalf of the Church without becoming, as we say nowadays, emotionally involved. But the amazing thing is that although always a sick man he could nevertheless conduct, as it were, a war with equal energy on two fronts at the same time while being quite as deeply involved in both. It seems scarcely credible yet it is true that while he was fighting the King of England heart and soul for the liberty of the York Chapter, he was at the same time fighting the King of France for precisely the same thing on behalf of the canons of Bourges.

Just as the trouble in Yorkshire began in the year 1141 with the election of a successor to the Archbishop of York, so the trouble in France began in the same year with the election of a successor to the Archbishop of Bourges. The King of France, Louis le Jeune, who wanted the see of Bourges for a toady of his named Carduc, promised the Chapter complete freedom of choice while at the same time vetoing the one acceptable candidate, Peter le Châtre. So far the situation was much the same as at York, but the difference was that the canons of Bourges were more strong-minded than their English brethren and, in defiance of the king, elected the candidate he had forbidden. Immediately afterwards Peter left for Rome where the Pope confirmed his election and, since probably none of the French bishops would have dared to perform the ceremony in view of the King's attitude, consecrated him Archbishop, remarking that the King was only a boy and should be taught manners. The King swore a public oath that so long as he lived Peter would never have possession of his see; Peter took refuge with Count Theobald of Champagne; and the Pope laid the King under an interdict. It was a dangerous situation and Bernard viewed it with grave anxiety. Believing the interdict to be a mistake and only likely to make the King more stubborn, which is precisely what it did, he wrote to his friends in curia asking them to use their influence to have it raised.

"For two things I cannot excuse the King," he wrote, "he took an unlawful oath and kept it unjustly. He did the last not willingly but because he is ashamed to do otherwise. As you well know, it is considered a disgrace amongst the French to break an oath however ill-advisedly it may have been taken, although no wise man can doubt that unlawful oaths ought not to be kept. Yet even so I cannot admit that he is to be excused in the matter. But I have undertaken to obtain pardon for him not to excuse him. It is for you to consider whether, on the grounds of his youth, anger, or position, he can be excused. He could be without doubt if you let mercy triumph over justice, taking into account that he is a mere youth, albeit a king, and thus deserving of leniency on the understanding that he will not presume on it in future. I would say: let him be spared if he can be without prejudice to the liberties of the Church, or to the reverence due to the archbishop who was consecrated by the Apostolic hands. This is what the King himself humbly begs for, and what our afflicted Church on this side of the Alps implores. Otherwise we join hands with death, pining and withering away for dread of what we fear will come upon the world."[1]

Most unfortunately, just when the King was about to submit on the matter of Bourges, an event occurred which caused the whole situation to flare up again and banished any immediate prospect of peace. In the year 1142 Count Ralph de Vermandois was excommunicated by a Council held at Lagny under the presidency of the Apostolic Legate for having repudiated his first wife Leonora, a niece of Count Theobald, and married Petronella a sister of the Queen of France; the count refused to submit and the King, under the influence of the Queen, supported him. Here indeed was a situation which if not carefully handled was fraught with danger and, as nearly always happens, it was bungled and the danger materialized into something far worse than could have been feared. The King laid waste the territory of Count Theobald, and his soldiery behaved with the utmost brutality, horrifying Europe by setting fire to the small village of Vitry and burning to death large numbers of the inhabitants.

The devout Count Theobald had no army to match the forces of the King, he only had the prayers of his monks to call upon, but the King refused to desist from his depredations until he had promised

[1] Ep. 293 (Migne 219).

to have the sentence of interdict and excommunication raised.
Bernard wrote to the Pope: "Distress and troubles are upon us!
The earth shivers and shakes at the death of men, the banishment of
the poor, and also the imprisonment of the rich. Religion itself is
being brought into contempt and shame. Even to mention peace
amongst us is counted a disgrace. That great lover of innocence and
piety, the Count Theobald, is almost at the mercy of his enemies.
. . . What more is there to say? So that the whole land should not
be laid waste, and the whole kingdom, being divided against itself,
fall, that most devoted son of yours and loving defender of the
liberties of the Church has been obliged under oath to have lifted
that sentence of excommunication and interdict which was promul-
gated by your legate Ivo of happy memory against the person and
territory of the tyrant who is the head and author of all these ills
and sorrows, and also against the adulteress. The aforesaid prince
did this at the entreaty and on the advice of loyal and wise men.
For they said it would be easy to obtain from you, without harm to
the Church, a renewal and irrevocable confirmation of the same
sentence which had been justly passed in the first place. Thus
artifice would be outwitted by artifice, and peace obtained without
the tyrant who 'takes pride in his own malice, in his own ill-doing'
gaining anything."[1]

Historians have severely blamed Bernard for what they describe
as the duplicity of the advice he mentions in the above letter, but it
should be noted that although he seems to have approved of it he
does not say that it originated from him or that he was wholly
responsible for it. Furthermore although it may have been bad
policy it is difficult to see how it can be condemned on moral
grounds. There was no question of condoning the adultery of
Ralph[2] but simply of lifting the punishment that had been imposed

[1] Ep. 295 (Migne 217).

[2] Very strangely at the Council of Rheims in 1148, presided over by the Cistercian
Pope Eugenius III and in the presence of St. Bernard, Count Ralph's marriage with
Petronella appears, according to John of Salisbury, to have been declared valid after
all and all that Bernard did was to say that no good would come of it. Thus John of
Salisbury: "Radulfus comes Veromannensis, qui trienno excommunicatus, eo quod
uxorem suam, quam injuste demiserat, absolutionem . . . fretus auxilio et consilio
diaconorum cardinalium, Joannis Paparonis et Gregorii de Sancto Angelo, obtinuit,
non sine suspicione intervenientis pecuniae . . . Interfuit vir sanctissimus dominus
Bernardus. Hic videns comitem Radulfum diu scandalizasse ecclesiam et adhuc in
contubernio a tribus apostolicis condemnato permanere dixit quod nusquam de lecto
illo soboles egressura quae laudabilem fructum faceret in populo Dei, et quod diu non
erant ad invicem gavisuri." Hist. Pont. Lib., vi and vii.

on him; the King did not insist that the second marriage should be sanctioned, merely that the penalty should be removed.

Besides writing to the Pope Bernard also addressed himself to the King: "God knows how fond of you I have always been ever since I first knew you, and how I have always wanted your honour. You, too, know with what anxiety and trouble I, with other faithful servants of yours, have striven during the last year to obtain peace for you." It will be remembered that Bernard had tried to persuade his friends in curia to have the interdict raised under which the Pope laid the King because of his behaviour over the Bourges election. He continues: "But I begin to fear that we have laboured in vain, for it is evident that you are too ready to kick aside frivolously and hastily the good and sound advice you receive; and, I know not under what devilish influence, to hasten back while their scars are still fresh to your former evil ways. . . . From whom but the devil himself could the advice come under which you are acting, which causes burnings upon burnings, and slaughter upon slaughter, and the voice of the poor and the groans of captives and the blood of the slain to echo in the ears of the Father of orphans and the Judge of Widows? Clearly the ancient enemy of our race is delighted with this hecatomb of slaughtered men, because 'he was a murderer from the beginning'. Do not try to 'cover up sin with smooth names' by citing Count Theobald as a futile pretext for your wrong doing, for he says that he is ready and indeed very willing to abide by the terms which were arranged between you both when peace was made, and that he is prepared to make immediate satisfaction in everything if those who love your name, that is to say the mediators between you both, should find him to have offended your honour in any way, which he does not think he has." From this it appears that, the Pope having lifted the sentence of interdict and excommunication as Bernard had suggested, some sort of peace treaty had been patched up, the terms of which the King was being reluctant to honour. Bernard now goes on to say what he thinks about his behaviour towards the Church: "But whatever you may be pleased to do with your own kingdom, and soul, we, the sons of the Church, cannot overlook the injuries, contempt and ignominy to which you have subjected our mother. . . . Certainly we shall make a stand and, if necessary, fight even to the death for our mother with the weapons that are permitted to us. . . . I now tell you that, provoked by the constant excesses you commit almost daily, I am beginning to regret having stupidly favoured your youth more than I should have done, and I am determined that in future to the best of my limited capacity, I shall expose the whole truth about you.

"I shall not withhold the fact that you are trying to make common cause with excommunicated persons, that I hear you are associating with robbers and thieves in the slaughter of men, the burning of homesteads, the destruction of churches, and the scattering of the poor. . . . I shall not conceal the fact that you have not even now corrected that unlawful and accursed oath you took against the church of Bourges; that you do not allow a pastor to care for the sheep of Christ at Châlons; and moreover that you billet your brother and his soldiers, archers, and cross-bowmen in the houses of the bishops against all right and justice, thereby rashly exposing the property of the Church to be squandered in disgraceful uses. I tell you, you will not remain long unpunished if you continue in this way."[1] In passing we might note another characteristic of Bernard borne out by this letter—his complete fearlessness.

At this juncture the situation was even further complicated by a most unhappy development. Ever since Bernard had taken up the defence of Peter of Pisa his relations with Pope Innocent had been strained, and now there occurred something in the nature of a complete rupture. Cardinal Ivo had lately died leaving Bernard one of his executors, and apparently the Pope was not satisfied with the way his property had been administered. Of course this was only a pretext, the Pope had long been tired of Bernard and resentful of his plain speaking; but for all that Bernard could not let the matter pass: "Now hear the plain truth," he wrote. "If I utter falsehood I shall be condemning myself out of my own mouth. When Cardinal Ivo put off his mortal body, I was absent, in fact I was very far away. But I heard from those who were present at the time that he made a will; and what he did he caused to be written down. He divided what he wished of his goods amongst those whom he wished, and what was left over he entrusted to two abbots who were then assisting him and to myself who was absent, to be distributed, because the poorer religious houses were known to us. When the abbots returned home and did not find me (I was detained at the time, according to your instructions, by the negotiations for peace) they nevertheless distributed the money as they thought best, not only

[1] Ep. 297 (Migne 221).

without my consent but also without my knowledge. Now, I beg you, let your anger give way before the truth . . .

"As for what I have heard about your displeasure at my many letters, there is no need for me to worry further about that for I can easily remedy it. . . ."[1]

By this time the King had become more amenable about Bourges and sent delegates to the Pope with instructions to accept any terms at all for the lifting of the interdict under which he was still living. But the Pope with all the obstinacy of a weak man refused these overtures of the King and sent his delegates home "*re infecta*"; on the top of this he threatened to reimpose the interdict on Count Ralph unless he separated from Petronella and went back to his first wife. Whereupon the King rounded on Bernard accusing him of treachery and began once more to devastate the territory of Count Theobald.

In desperation Count Theobald called a council of his friends. Things could hardly have looked blacker for him, he was completely at the King's mercy. Nevertheless Bernard, in his prophetic role, was able to assure him that within five weeks his trouble would be over, and so it turned out. On 24th September, 1143, Pope Innocent died and Bernard immediately wrote to his successor, Celestine II: "Count Theobald is a son of peace and what he asks for, I ask for too. He has a great zeal for peace, but asks you to carry it into effect. Yours is an apostolate of peace . . . all men desire it, few deserve it. But if neither the count nor myself deserve it, the plight of the Church demands it. The care of all the churches belongs solely to the Apostolic See that they may all be united under her and in her; its charge is to preserve the unity of all in the bonds of peace. Give us peace, send us peace. . . . Although we may not deserve it, you owe it to the Church."[2] This letter had its effect; the Pope greeted the delegates of the King warmly and lifted the interdict of his predecessor. It now only remained to settle the terms of peace. A council was held in the year 1144 at which the King was present; unfortunately, however, someone injured his *amour propre* by suggesting that he had been forced into an untenable position by bad advice, and he immediately stormed out of the council-chamber. "We lost almost all hope at the conference we lately had together at Corbeil," Bernard wrote to him. "You know how unreasonably (if you will pardon my saying so) you withdrew from us on that

[1] Ep. 292 (Migne 218).
[2] Ep. 304 (Migne 358).

occasion. Your annoyance allowed us no opportunity for clearly explaining what had displeased you in our discourse. If you had deigned to wait calmly for this, even you might perhaps have recognized that nothing was said unbecoming or unsupportable to you, in the present state of affairs."[1] How his times spring to life in the letters of Bernard! We can almost see the anxious statesmen sitting round while the young King storms and rants and leaves the room in fury with the Queen, his evil genius, lurking behind the scenes to know how things had gone.

After receiving the above letter the King consented to hold another peace conference and this time Queen Eleanor was present. Bernard did not miss this opportunity; he took the Queen aside and sternly rebuked her for misusing her influence over the King on behalf of Count Ralph and Petronella to the great hurt of both Church and State. It was not to be expected that the Queen could withstand the impetus of a personality before which even the Emperor Lothair had given way. She meekly explained that she had been embittered by her inability to bear children to her husband, whereupon Bernard promised her that if she would in future use her influence over the King to better purpose he would pray that she might have a child: a year later she bore the King a daughter; so at last peace came to the Church in France.

[1] Ep. 302 (Migne 226).

CHAPTER XVIII

On the fifteenth day of February in the year 1145 Bernard Paganelli, the Cistercian abbot of SS. Vincent and Anastasius, was elected Pope in succession to Lucius II and took the name of Eugenius. When the news reached Clairvaux Bernard was overwhelmed and bewildered. "God have mercy on you; what have you done?" he wrote to the cardinals in curia. "You have recalled a dead man from the grave and restored him to his fellow men. You have plunged once more into the world and the cares of the world a man who had fled from both. A man crucified to the world has been brought back to the world by you, and a man who 'had chosen to lie forgotten in the house of the Lord' you have set up to be the lord of all men. . . . What reason made you, as soon as the late Pope had died, suddenly rush upon this rustic, lay hands upon him when he was in hiding from the world, knock away his axe, mattock, or hoe, drag him to the Palatine, and clothe him in fine linen and purple? Had you no other wise and experienced man amongst you who would have been better suited for these things? It seems ridiculous to take a man in rags and make him preside over princes, command bishops, and dispose of kingdoms and empires. Ridiculous or miraculous? It could be either." Plainly Bernard was moved and even excited by the news, yet he had no illusions about this monk of his who had become Pope, for he goes on to say: "And yet I am not happy in my own mind about your choice, for he has a sensitive and diffident nature and he is not accustomed to dealing in great affairs. I fear he may not exercise the Apostolate with sufficient firmness."[1] But to the new Pope himself Bernard wrote in a rather different vein: " 'As cold water to a thirsty soul, so is good tidings from a far country.' When your letter bearing upon it your seal was unrolled, from the fulness thereof we all received good tidings, words of consolation, the greeting and apostolic benediction. When I heard the news that it contained my spirit came to life within me and I cast myself on the ground in thanks to God, and all of us, your brothers, cast ourselves on the ground."[2] Well indeed

[1] Ep. 315 (Migne 237).
[2] Ep. 314. The original published by Hüffer.

might Bernard "cast himself on the ground in thanks to God" for to have one of his Cistercians on the throne of Peter meant, or might well mean, the triumph of all his ideals, of all he had stood for and spent himself for during the last thirty years. The small and insignificant monastery which he had entered just thirty-two years before had become, largely owing to his own dynamic personality, the mother house of a huge and prosperous Order spread throughout the world; the small mustard seed had become a great tree and men of all nations were taking refuge under its shade. In electing one of his monks to be the Pope the Church had done more than merely set her seal of approval on Bernard's ideals and activities, she had set Bernard of Clairvaux as much as Bernard Paganelli to rule over her, so that he would soon be writing to Pope Eugenius: "Men are saying it is not you but I who am the Pope, and from all sides they are flocking to me with their suits."[1]

We have reached the final phase of Bernard's life. He was fifty-four years of age and at the zenith of his powers. His name had become a household word as far off as the Court of King David in Scotland and the fortress of the Kings of Jerusalem in Palestine. He numbered his sons in every country of Europe and in every court his lightest word commanded respect even when it did not compel obedience. Everyone came to him with their troubles, kings and princes, bishops and priests, the Pope himself sat at his feet, and there was no one so insignificant and poor that could not count on his protection and help. He dealt in great affairs of state, but no trouble was too small to claim his attention. He answered all his letters even from the most humble people and he was as ready to champion the cause of a poor man who had lost his pigs as of a Pope that had lost his throne. Very soon now he would be carrying the whole world of his time upon his shoulders and hurling it against the Saracen in defence of the Holy Places in Palestine.

It were futile to judge the crusades by the standards and prejudices of the twentieth century; we shall never understand them unless we try to appreciate the ideals that lay behind them and look at them from the point of view of the age that gave them birth. It was an age in love with order and, because it was also an age of faith, the only order it knew was the Christian Order; beyond this was only confusion and darkness, and within it Christ's vicar upon earth was the Pope, to whom, in theory, all things were directly or indirectly

[1] Ep. 206 (Migne 239).

subordinate. "He presides over princes, commands bishops, and disposes of kingdoms and empires,"[1] wrote Bernard. The Pope's hand held two swords: the temporal and the spiritual, the latter to be wielded by himself and the former at his command by the Emperor in defence of the Church or, what amounted to almost the same thing in those days, Christendom. The shrine or sacred territory of this Christian order was the land made holy by the life of Christ, and above all the sacred city of Jerusalem. Bernard might and, in fact, did counsel the Pope to leave Rome[2] but neither he nor his contemporaries could ever contemplate relinquishing Jerusalem; it was the spiritual home of every Christian. To understand this point of view more clearly we cannot do better than study the encyclical letter Bernard sent to all the nations that he could not visit personally in order to stir them to take up arms in the crusade. "I address myself to you," he wrote to the English people, "in the cause of Christ, in whom lies our salvation. I am a person of small account, but my love for you in Christ is not small. This is my reason for writing to you, this is why I make bold to address myself to you. I would have preferred to do so by word of mouth had I but the strength to come to you.

"Now is the acceptable time, now is the day of abundant salvation. The earth is shaken because the Lord of heaven is losing his land, the land in which he appeared to men, in which he lived amongst men for more than thirty years; the land made glorious by his miracles, holy by his blood; the land in which the flowers of his resurrection first blossomed. And now, for our sins, the enemy of the cross has begun to lift his sacrilegious head there, and to devastate with the sword that blessed land, that land of promise. Alas, if there should be none to withstand him, he will soon invade the very city of the living God, overturn the arsenal of our redemption, and defile the holy places which have been adorned by the blood of the immaculate lamb. They have cast their greedy eyes especially on the holy sanctuaries of our Christian religion, and they long especially to violate that couch on which, for our sakes, the Lord of life fell asleep in death.

"What are you doing, you mighty men of valour? What are you doing, you servants of the cross? Will you thus cast holy things to dogs, pearls before swine? How great a number of sinners have

[1] Ep. 315 (Migne 237).
[2] De Consideratione Lib. cap. iii.

here confessed with tears and obtained pardon for their sins since the time when these holy precincts were cleansed of pagan filth by the swords of our fathers? The evil one sees this and is enraged, he gnashes his teeth and withers away in fury. He stirs up his vessels of wrath so that if they do but once lay hands upon these holy places there shall be no sign or trace of piety left. Such a catastrophe would be a source of appalling grief for all time, but it would also be a source of confusion and boundless shame for our generation."[1]

But a crusade was no ordinary war, it was something more in the nature of a pilgrimage and the most efficacious way of expiating crimes. After saying that of course God could summon countless legions of angels for the defence of his land, Bernard continues: "But he has pity on this generation and on those who have grievously fallen away and has prepared for them a means of salvation. Consider with what care he plans our salvation, and be amazed. Look, sinners, at the depths of his pity, and take courage. When almighty God so treats murderers, thieves, adulterers, perjurers, and such like as persons able to find righteousness in his service, what is it but an act of exquisite courtesy all God's own? God is good, and were he intent on your punishment he would not have asked of you this service, or indeed have accepted it had you offered it."[2] Very fine indeed, but it may be doubted whether "murderers, thieves, adulterers" make ideal recruits for such a project as this; yet Bernard was incapable of believing that anyone could undertake it but for the highest motives.

In the year 1145 during his coronation celebrations at Bourges King Louis revealed to the assembled nobles the secret desire of his heart to lead a crusade in defence of the Holy Land. On the face of it the situation there was ripe for something of the sort; it had been deteriorating ever since the death of Fulk of Anjou in 1143 and only in the previous year Edessa, the gateway to Jerusalem, had fallen to Zengi; moreover a crusade was probably as good a way as any for young Louis to retrieve the good name he had lost in brutally devastating the territory of Count Theobald. Nevertheless the idea was not received with all the enthusiasm that he desired; men were moved to tears by his words, but they were not willing to be moved any further. Suger was openly opposed to it; the loyalty of some of the great vassals was doubtful and he feared they might

---

[1] Ep. 391. MS. 14845 fol. 257. Bibliothèque Nationale, Paris.
[2] Ibid.

seize the opportunity of the King's absence for revolting. On the other hand the Pope gave it his unqualified approval and delegated Bernard to preach it in his place since he had his hands full in Rome at the time. As we can imagine, the crusade exerted a powerful appeal over Bernard and stirred in his veins the blood of his warrior ancestors; until the project had received the Pope's approval he had refused to have anything to do with it, but now he was ready and willing to support it with all his boundless energy and eloquence. A great meeting was arranged for Palm Sunday, 31st March, 1146, at Vezelay which Bernard would open with a sermon.

It is not hard to picture that wonderful Sunday morning at Vezelay, a city set upon a hill and crowned with its great church soaring into the clouds above the smiling plains of Burgundy: all the glory and colour of the Middle Ages, the King with his retinue of counsellors and noblemen, bishops and statesmen in their robes and gay accoutrements, and the cheerful noise of a crowd on holiday, then a tense silence as the tall and emaciated figure of Bernard mounted the rostrum. As his voice echoed through the crowds, tearing at men's hearts and stirring their courage, his figure became transformed and his face shone so that men thought they were listening to an angel from heaven. The strain became too great; the people could not contain themselves; applause and shouts of "To Jerusalem" broke out, and then silence once more while the young King came forward to kneel in front of the preacher and receive the cross. A moving and wonderful scene, but it was only the beginning. Bernard traversed the provinces and everywhere men flocked to receive the cross from his hands, and miracles of every sort and kind lent wonder to his flaming words. In a few months he could write to the Pope: "You have ordered and I have obeyed, and your authority has made my obedience fruitful, towns and castles are emptied, one may scarcely find one man amongst seven women . . ."[1] Always the same Bernard, the whole world hanging on his words yet never anything in his own eyes but himself the least of men, the worst of sinners. "Your authority has made my obedience fruitful"—this to Eugenius who could not keep his own Roman rabble in order! Perhaps the greatest of all Bernard's miracles was his humility.

In the meantime messengers had arrived from Roger of Sicily to offer the King of France supplies for the expedition and the personal

[1] Ep. 323 (Migne 347).

co-operation of either himself or his son. The rulers of Hungary and Germany also promised assistance and the Basileus Manuel wrote a fulsome letter of encouragement. The hopes of Christendom soared, all Europe sounded with the rustle of drawing swords, men dreamed dreams of valour and saw all the riches of the East at their feet. At this point an unfortunate incident occurred: a certain monk, apparently a Cistercian but a rude and uneducated fellow, began wandering round the Rhineland inciting the excited crowds to take the cross and begin the crusade by setting about the Jews. Bernard was dismayed at the news: "The fellow you mention in your letter," he wrote to the Archbishop of Mainz, "has received no authority from men or through men, nor has he been sent by God. If he makes himself out to be a monk or a hermit, and on that score claims liberty to preach and the duty of doing so, he can and should know that the first duty of a monk is not to preach but to pray. He is clearly a fellow without sense and devoid of all modesty! A fellow whose foolishness has been set upon a candlestick for all the world to see! I find three things most reprehensible in him: unauthorized preaching, contempt for episcopal authority, and incitement to murder. Is it not a far better triumph for the Church to convince and convert the Jews than to put them all to the sword? Has that prayer which the Church offers for the Jews that the veil may be drawn from their hearts so that they may be led from the darkness of error into the light of truth, been instituted in vain? What horrid learning, what hellish doctrine this man teaches. His is a foul heresy, a sacrilegious prostitution 'pregnant with malice, that has conceived only spite and given birth only to shame'. I should like to say more but I must forbear. To sum up briefly what I feel about this man, I should say that he was a man with a great opinion of himself and full of arrogance. He shows by his works and teaching that he would like to make a great name for himself, but is without the ability to do so."[1] The Jews of that district have never forgotten Bernard's protection of their race and to this day they sometimes name their children after him as a sign of their gratitude.

After this Bernard set out again on his travels, preaching the crusade everywhere he went and supporting his words with so many miracles that the diary of the two monks Gerard and Geoffrey, who accompanied him, came to be known as the Book of Miracles. In the Autumn he set out for Flanders, pausing at Arras on the way

[1] Ep. 393 (Migne 365).

to attend a council of abbots and bishops; from there he went to Bruges by way of Ypres and by the middle of October he was at Villers, a daughter house of Clairvaux. From here he set out to Germany to win over the Emperor Conrad and preach the crusade to the people. It would be tedious to follow his whole itinerary through Germany and it would add very little to our knowledge of his character to do so. He had left Clairvaux early in the Autumn of 1146 and he did not get back there until the Spring of the following year; during all this time he was traversing the cities and countryside of Germany preaching and everywhere it was the same story; wherever he went he was received as a messenger of God and the enthusiasm of the crowd knew no bounds. Sometimes he even had to be rescued from their rather excited and violent demonstrations in his honour and on one occasion at least the Emperor Conrad himself had to push through the crowds and carry him off to safety in his arms. The only opposition he seems to have encountered was from Conrad himself, who at first was not at all in favour of the crusade and told Bernard very bluntly that he had no intention of participating. But at Spires, where a tradition uncorroborated by evidence says that Bernard added the final three invocations to the "*Salve Regina*", during a Mass of the Holy Ghost, Bernard addressed him personally in a public sermon urging him to take the cross in gratitude to God for his favours to him, with the result that he changed his mind and declared himself willing to serve God with his sword as Bernard suggested.

There is no doubt at all that Bernard's mission on behalf of the crusade in Germany was a spectacular success, the popular appeal of his personality seems to have been quite irresistible, yet his mandate from the Pope does not seem to have extended beyond France and it is permissible to regret that he did not keep to it. Had he done so the story of the crusade might have been different, for the innate hostility between the two races was one of the rocks on which it came to grief. But it were easier to curb a river in spate than to shackle Bernard by petty considerations of policy when once his emotions and enthusiasm were involved; such considerations did not come within his horizon and would have been quite alien to his nature; it was God's work and that was enough for him.

On 16th February in the year 1147 Bernard attended the council at Etampes to settle the final preparations, the route which the armies would take and, a very important matter, who should govern France during the absence of the King. Bernard persuaded the King and all the counsellors to leave Suger, the Abbot of St. Denis, and the Count of Nevers in charge; "Here are two swords and it is enough," he said. After this he was once again on his travels passing through Maisse, Milly, and Morel on his way to Sens, and then on again to Chablis, and Tonnerre, everywhere and to everyone preaching the crusade and distributing the crosses. He was back again at Clairvaux by the end of the month but by the middle of March he was at Frankfort to attend the diet convoked by Conrad in order to consider how best to protect the frontiers of Germany against the invasions of the Slavs while he was absent. It was decided that the princes, prelates and people of Moravia should have the high duty of either converting or exterminating these peoples and that by doing this they would share in the privileges and blessings of the crusaders in Palestine. Bernard was delegated to write to them: "We utterly forbid," he wrote, "that for any reason whatsoever a truce should be made with these peoples, until such a time as, by God's help, they shall either be converted or wiped out."[1]

Everything was now ready for the first act in the tragedy. In May 1147 a large contingent of, so it is said, 100,000 men left Bamberg under the leadership of the Emperor Conrad; in June the King of France was ready to depart. Before going Louis presented himself at the Abbey of St. Denis to commend his country to the care of its patron Saint during his absence and to beg his blessing on the venture. In the presence of the Pope, who had been obliged to leave Rome for a time, and surrounded by his court he prostrated himself before the shrine and kissed the relics of the Saint, then having received from the hands of the Pope the sacred oriflamme and the pilgrim's staff he was ready to depart. Surrounded by the monks of the community, by his mother and wife and all his court, he bade them farewell. It was a touching and impressive scene and many wept at the sight of it; but the King would have done better to have left his Queen and womenfolk behind him in the care of Saint Denis; as it was, they followed him on the campaign and were the cause of numerous rather undignified scenes and complications. Nevertheless everyone and most of all Bernard was full of confidence: it was the work of God and could not fail.

As all the world knows the second crusade was a complete fiasco. By July of 1148 Christendom was horror-struck by the news that

[1] Ep. 394 (Migne 467).

the siege of Damascus had been raised, then slowly news of further disasters filtered through followed by the remnants of the conquered armies. Everyone turned on Bernard; he had preached the crusade, he had promised the blessing of God on it, and now it had failed. Bernard was heart-broken and poured out his anguish to the Pope: "Now the heathen are saying, 'Where is their God?' and no wonder, for our armies have perished in the desert or by the sword or from starvation; our princes have quarrelled, and fear, misery, and confusion have seeped into their kingdoms. I promised peace and there has been no peace, I promised good things and behold there has only been trouble! It is as if I had been rash or fickle, yet I acted under obedience to you or rather to God through you. Why has God ignored our fasts and turned a deaf ear to our prayers? We know his judgements are true, but this judgement of his on us is exceeding difficult and I should not hesitate to call that man blessed who is not scandalized by it.

"Yet if the Israelites fell in battle and perished because of their wickedness can we be surprised if we who have sinned in the same way should suffer the same fate? Nevertheless the Israelites did not lose heart, their faith was strong in proportion that their power in war was weak. God said to them, 'Go up to battle,' and they went up to battle and were again defeated. First with the consent of God and then by his command they gave battle and yet were worsted. What would our people think of me if they gave battle again at my suggestion and again succumbed? Yet the Israelites after they had been defeated twice gave battle a third time and were victorious. Perhaps our people would ask me what signs I could give to prove that my words were of God? It is not for me to answer this; do you spare my modesty and answer for me according to what you have been told and seen with your own eyes. Yet it is nothing to me that I should be blamed by those who cannot tell the difference between good and evil. It were better that men should grumble against me than against God."[1] Beyond the revelation it gives of Bernard's agony at the outcome of the crusade and his indomitable courage in advising a second attempt the interest of the above passage lies in the reference he makes to his own miracles. In fact Bernard did all he could to encourage another attempt. "I tell you," he wrote to the Pope, "such a grave and universal crisis is no time for half-hearted and timid measures; 'he is no brave man whose courage

[1] De Consideratione. Lib. ii, cap. 1.

does not rise in face of difficulty'."[1] But, in spite of the support of Suger and Peter the Venerable, the project came to nothing, nor did Bernard ever completely recover his prestige and popularity afterwards. Like so many great Saints and like the King and Pattern of true Sanctity, his life ended under the cloud of apparent failure.

It is not within the scope of this book to deal at length with the reasons for the failure of the second crusade. Briefly it may be said to have arisen from the complete ignorance of Bernard and the West in general of the true situation. They had no appreciation of the role of Byzantium in maintaining civilization and peace in the East, nor of the hardly ill-founded suspicions entertained by the Basileus of the intentions of the West in general and Count Roger of Sicily in particular.[2] There was also rivalry and petty jealousy amongst the leaders. Furthermore the project was organized on too vast a scale for the technical equipment of the age; a smaller and more highly trained force would have had better hope of success. Finally, as we have seen, Bernard himself was quite incapable of understanding how anyone could undertake the crusade for any but the highest motive and apparently quite unaware of the danger inherent in the promiscuous recruitment of all the riff-raff of Europe.

[1] Ep. 399 (Migne 256).
[2] When the project of the crusade was first mooted the Basileus Manuel was planning an attack on Roger of Sicily with the assistance of the Emperor Conrad.

CHAPTER XIX

In the year 1148 just before the raising of the siege of Damascus but shortly after the French army had been decimated before Antioch, Bernard found himself embroiled in a sharp doctrinal controversy. A certain Gilbert de la Porrée, one of the most learned men of his day, had been causing anxiety to such men as Peter Lombard and Abbot Suger as well as to Bernard by his novel teaching on the Trinity and by the distinction he seemed to make between deity and God; and during the month of April he was summoned to answer for his doctrine to the Pope in council at Rheims. John of Salisbury, at one time a disciple of Gilbert, has given us an account of what happened.[1] Before the consistory had met Bernard summoned to his rooms certain bishops and abbots and other churchmen, including Peter Lombard, Abbot Suger of St. Denis, Calo who became Bishop of Poitiers, and Robert Melun who became Bishop of Hereford, to consider the import of Gilbert's teaching. After declaring that it was the duty of bishops to remove scandals from the Church and begging them to correct him if he were mistaken in anything as it was no business of a monk to judge of such matters, Bernard read out certain statements to which he asked their approval; some of the clergy present objected to this method but did not say anything for fear of offending him. He obtained the consent of the assembly to the statements that the three persons of the Trinity are God and the converse, and that the essence and substance of God became incarnate, but when he asked them to agree that God was simple and that whatever was in God was God and that the properties of the persons were the persons themselves so that the Father was paternity, the Son filiality, and the Holy Spirit procession and the converse, the Archdeacon of Châlons, Robert de Bosco, got up and begged them not to be too hasty in agreeing to this statement but to wait until they had the Pope and cardinals present because many learned men of the day, including Anselm and Ralph of Laon, had rejected it.

When the cardinals heard of this meeting called by Bernard they were furious and said that this was just how he had attacked Peter

[1] Joan. Sal. Historia Pontificalis Lib. viii-xiv.

Abelard; but, as John of Salisbury says and as indeed we can well suppose, many of them were very jealous of him and quite ready to snatch at the smallest opportunity to calumniate him. Bernard went at once to the Pope and put his point of view to him and the Pope according to John of Salisbury was in entire sympathy with him for Bernard was a man "mighty in word and deed with God as some say and with men as we all have reason to know".[1] Soon afterwards Gilbert duly presented himself before the Pope and his council, surrounded by the clergy of his household carrying great volumes of the Fathers of the Church. Quite confident in the support of the cardinals he hotly defended his case arguing at length and quoting liberally from the Greek and Latin Fathers. This meeting seems to have ended inconclusively, but when on the following day or soon afterwards Gilbert was confronted by the Pope with certain statements he had made in his commentary on the "*De Trinitate*" of Boetius he declared himself perfectly willing to alter anything he had said of which the Pope disapproved, only begging that he might be allowed to make the corrections himself; whereupon the Pope instructed him to bring his book into line with the statements which Bernard had enunciated previously at the meeting he had called. This Gilbert humbly agreed to do, thereby escaping formal condemnation, but there were many who said he was not sincere and had not the smallest intention of doing any such thing.

Some time afterwards John of Salisbury suggested to Gilbert that he should meet Bernard privately and discuss the doctrine of St. Hilary on which he claimed to base his teaching. Gilbert haughtily replied that there had been discussion enough and that if Bernard wanted to understand the writings of St. Hilary he should first seek instruction in the liberal arts and other preliminary matters. "They were both very learned men but in quite different subjects," John of Salisbury comments. Some years previously[2] Bernard had befriended John of Salisbury and written on his behalf to Theobald, Archbishop of Canterbury: "I am sending to your Highness John, the bearer of this letter. He is a friend of mine and of my friends and I beg that he may benefit from your friendship. He has a good reputation amongst good men, not less for his life than for his learning. If I have any influence with you, and I know that I have

[1] Ibid.
[2] There is some doubt about the exact date of this letter.

much, provide for him that he may have the means to live decently and honourably, and I beg of you to do this without delay for he has nowhere to turn."[1] Here surely we see Bernard at his best, a very different man from the dour ascetic of popular opinion. Although one of the most busy men in Europe he could find time to take an interest in the welfare of a poor and, as yet, almost unknown English scholar, so that he might be able to live "decently and honourably".

The declining years of Bernard were saddened by the death of many friends, a common enough experience for all those who live to old age but especially poignant for Bernard who gave all his heart to his friends. In the year 1148 he lost the dearest of them all, the Irishman Saint Malachy of Armagh. They had first met when Malachy visited Clairvaux in the year 1139 on his way to Rome. An intimate friendship immediately sprang up between them: "Sinner though I be," wrote Bernard of their first meeting, "I found favour in his eyes and our friendship endured until his death as strong as it had been in the beginning."[2] Malachy for his part was so impressed by all that he saw at Clairvaux that he asked the Pope for permission to lay down his charge and become a monk there, and when this was refused he called there on his way back and left behind him four of his companions so that they could be formed in the Cistercian way of life and introduce it to Ireland on their return. As soon as he got back to Ireland he sent another small group to join them with a staff, perhaps of Irish blackthorn, as a gift to Bernard. "Amongst the many worries and troubles by which I am distracted," Bernard wrote to him, "your brethren from a distant land, your letter, and your gift of a staff are my comfort. Your letter proves your good will, your staff supports my weak body, and your brothers serve God humbly. . . . With regard to your wish that I should send you two of the brothers to prepare a place, I have discussed it with the brethren and we are agreed that it would not be well for them to be separated from us until Christ is more fully formed in them, until they are better equipped to fight for the Lord. . . . Do you in the meantime, with the wisdom given you by the Lord, look for and prepare a site similar to what you have seen here, far removed from the turmoil of the world. . . ."[3] When at last the brethren did return things do not seem to have gone very

---

[1] Ep. 389 (Migne 361).
[2] Vita S. Malachiae, c. xvi.
[3] Ep. 383 (Migne 341).

easily at first. The natives of Ireland appear to have objected to their
"French ways", and in another letter to Malachy Bernard refers to
"those natives of your country who are little disciplined and find it
hard to obey observances that are strange to them",[1] but nevertheless seven Cistercian houses were founded in the ten years that followed the foundation of Mellifont in 1142. Nine years after his
first visit Malachy was at Clairvaux once more, but this time he
came to die. He arrived an old and tired man and on the feast of
St. Luke, 18th October, he took to his bed, "and," wrote Bernard,
"all the house fell sick with him." Two weeks later soon after mid-
night on 2nd November, he died. "If we had here an abiding city,"
wrote Bernard to the brethren in Ireland, "we might rightly shed
tears at the loss of such a fellow-citizen as Malachy; and if we look,
as we should, for one that is to come, the loss of such a valuable
leader will still be an occasion for sorrow, yet nevertheless in this
case knowledge should moderate our feelings and sure hope set a
limit to our grief. We would prove ourselves not only wanting in
charity but also ungrateful for all that we have received through
him, were we not glad for his sake that he has passed from his many
labours to everlasting repose, from the dangers of this world to the
safety of heaven. . . . Even considerations of our own advantage
suggest that we should rejoice and be glad that we have such a
powerful patron in the court of heaven, a faithful advocate whose
deep love will not permit him to forget us. . . . The Lord has highly
honoured us by favouring our house with the blessed death of
Malachy and enriching it with the treasure of his blessed body. Do
not take it ill that he should have his tomb with us, since God out
of his abundant mercy has so ordained it that you should have him
while he lived and we when he was dead. For both you and us he
was a common father, and still is, for this was the wish he expressed
to us on his death-bed."[2] Bernard's *Life of Malachy* is a work of
piety and edification, but it is nevertheless interesting for the glimpse
it gives of the barbarous and rude manners prevalent in Ireland at
that date. He tells us in it how Malachy, "who derived no more ill
effects from his barbarian birth and education than a fish does from
the salt water in which it lives",[3] "restored amongst his people the
most salutary use of confession, the sacrament of confirmation, and

[1] Ep. 385 (Migne 357).
[2] Ep. 386 (Migne 374).
[3] Vita S. Mal., c. i.

the marriage contract, of all of which the people were either ignorant or negligent".[1]

In the year 1150 at a council called to consider the possibility of another crusade Bernard was chosen to lead the expedition. "I expect you must have heard by now," he wrote to the Pope, "how the assembly at Chartres, by a most surprising decision, chose me as the leader of the expedition. You may be quite sure that this never was and is not by my advice or wish, and that it is altogether beyond my powers, as I gauge them, to do such a thing. I could think of nothing more remote from my calling, even supposing I had the necessary strength and skill."[2] The plan came to nothing.

On 13th January in the following year Bernard's friend Abbot Suger died. Bernard had written to him on his death-bed: "Fear not, man of God, to put off this muddy vesture of decay that is holding you down to the earth. Why trouble about your clothing of flesh when you are about to put on the garb of immortality in heaven? I am torn, dear friend, by the desire to come and see you, that I may receive a dying man's blessing. But no man can arrange his life just as he pleases, and so I cannot dare to promise what I am not sure of being able to perform; yet I will try my best to do what I am not yet able to see my way to doing. But whatever happens I, who have loved you from the first, shall love you without end. Be mindful of me when you come to where I shall follow you, so that I may be permitted soon to come after you and come to you. In the meantime be sure that I shall never lose the dear memory of you, although to my sorrow I lose your dear presence. Yet God can keep you with us in answer to our prayers, he can still preserve you for those who need you, of this there can be no doubt."[3]

During the winter of 1152 Bernard took to his bed so ill that it seemed as if he would never rise again, but in the following Spring he rallied and set off on a long journey to Metz in order to make peace between the Bishop of that town and the Duke of Lorraine. There had been open warfare between them and thousands of the people of Metz had been caught in a defile and slaughtered. The Archbishop of Trèves arrived at Clairvaux to implore Bernard to intervene. Although he was desperately ill he did not hesitate but rose from his bed and set off immediately. He found the two armies

[1] Vita S. Mal., c. iii.
[2] Ep. 399 (Migne 256).
[3] Ep. 411 (Migne 266).

opposing each other on the banks of the Moselle; the Messines intent on revenge refused even to hear what Bernard had to say, and their opponents rejected his proposals out of hand, but Bernard was not disheartened and assured his companions that peace would come. Finally a meeting was arranged by Bernard; peace of a sort was arranged between the belligerents so that he could return home with the sense of having achieved something, although unfortunately what he had achieved did not last.

Soon after Bernard's return to Clairvaux news reached him that Pope Eugenius had died, but Bernard himself had only a month longer to live. He fell sick again almost as soon as he got back from Metz and on Thursday, 20th August in the year 1153, shortly after receiving the last sacraments, surrounded by his grief-stricken monks he died, and with his death the Middle Ages went into a slow decline.

CHAPTER XX

It is not easy for us to conceive a clear idea of the appearance or character of a twelfth-century Saint; the whole idiom of those days is so very different to ours. When we possess a contemporary picture it is too idealized to provide us with any idea of what he looked like, and when we possess a contemporary description, as we do in Bernard's case, we are not helped by it because the purpose of such descriptions was to edify rather than to inform; only virtues and miracles are mentioned, and the result is a flat and lifeless picture like a badly over-exposed photograph with no high-lights because there are no shadows.

How, for instance, are we to understand the phrase that Bernard's eyes were "dove-like"? Does this mean that his eyes were pink or red like the eyes of an albino? More probably it simply means that the expression of his eyes was gentle, but it is very hard to be certain. We can, however, safely assume that by the standards of the day he was exceptionally handsome, but tastes differ from age to age and even from country to country, and as we cannot be certain about the taste in this matter of the twelfth century it is not easy to imagine what Bernard looked like. His hair was certainly reddish brown, like his father's, and he would have been bearded; he was tall for the time, probably about five foot ten, and his colouring was rather high. That is all we can say about his appearance.

We have more ample grounds on which to form a judgement of his character; there are his actions, the biographies of his friends, his writings and, above all, his letters, not all of his letters by any means, but probably all that his contemporaries wished us to have, and a few more that escaped their censorship.

In estimating the character of Bernard we must never forget that he was always a sick man and probably nearly always in pain. It is difficult to know exactly what ailed him, but it was undoubtedly some grievous gastric complaint, possibly consumption as well. It was only the grace of God, a strong will, and an incredible vitality that kept him going. From his earliest youth he had also suffered from severe headaches, probably megrims, and there is no doubt that he was nervous and abnormally highly strung, but this is not to say that his nerves got on top of him; on the contrary owing to his vital spiritual life, he seems to have been as perfectly integrated and self-controlled as any man can hope to be. But the fact remains that he was a highly strung, emotional, and even passionate man. It is also worth bearing in mind that he seems to have been abnormally devoted to his mother and to have felt parting with her in order to go to school at Châtillon very severely, and we know that her death was a terrible shock for him.

Granted a temperament like his, informed and sublimated by the grace of God, Bernard's fierce and uncompromising asceticism is no matter for surprise. The gentle humanism of Cluny would have been quite impossible for him; his was a nature that must go to extremes. He was not one of those who could use the good and beautiful things of the world calmly and innocently; for him they were a real danger, a real source of emotional upheaval, he could not use them without being captured by them and enslaved. The wonderful carvings, jewels, and ornaments of Cluny were a real source of distraction to him. Probably he could never have got used to them; he was too susceptible to physical beauty. When, in the early days of Clairvaux, he told his novices to leave their bodies outside the door, he was only telling them to do what he had been obliged to do himself. But there is ample evidence that experience made him far more tolerant and sympathetic, if not more understanding. No one could be kinder and more helpful than Bernard when he had once learned that not all monks were made like himself, and he learned this hard lesson quickly.

Bernard's tender devotion to Our Blessed Lady and the humanity of Christ is well known; it was in this way that he sublimated his sensibility. It is a mistake to say that devotion to Our Blessed Lady was Bernard's method of countering Courtly Love, because it did not appear until half a century after his death; it would be more true to say that Courtly Love was a secularization of Bernard's devotion to Our Blessed Lady. It would perhaps be true to say that Bernard found in Our Lady an object for the love he always had for his mother, but we must beware of exaggeration and sentimentalizing. It is true that Bernard did have a great love for Our Lady, but we must not attribute to him an attitude that is to be found only in his spurious works; his was a reasoned love.

It is sometimes said that Bernard completely mortified his sensibility by asceticism; this is not true. He did not, so we are told, notice the vaulting of the roof at Citeaux or the Lake of Geneva as he rode by it, but this was because of his enormous power of recollection and prayer. It is perfectly clear from his treatise on Humility and Pride that not the smallest human weakness escaped him when he wanted to see, and apparently he noticed the decorations of the Abbey Church of Cluny well enough. He guided and disciplined his sensibility but he did not kill it.

Bernard's genius for friendship and the whole-hearted love he gave to his friends is well in keeping with what we know of his character. Men of those days were far less inhibited and self-conscious than we are in their expression of affection because, no doubt, they were more innocent and, perhaps, more ignorant of the psychological implications. The cult of friendship was a feature of the day, and the nature of true love was a common subject for speculation. Cicero's treatise on Friendship was widely read in monasteries and St. Aelred of Rievaulx wrote a Christian, one might almost say monastic version of it. The modern pseudopsychologist may well raise his eyebrows, but the truth is this open and simple recognition of friendship between men and the high store laid by it was far more innocent and healthy than the furtive and self-conscious relationship to which modern psychology ill-understood threatens to reduce it nowadays. Thus Bernard could write to his great friend William of St. Thierry who was worried because he felt that his love for him was not reciprocated: "What proof have you that my affection for you is less than yours is for me? Is it, as you aver in the postscript of your letter, that the messengers from here who pass to and fro by you never bring any token of my goodwill or affection? What sort of token, what sort of proof do you expect? . . . O Lord who searchest the hearts of men! O Sun of Justice, whose rays enlighten the hearts of men with divers graces! Thou knowest and I feel that by thy gift I love this man for the sake of his goodness. But how much I love him, that I cannot tell, thou knowest. It is thou, Lord, who givest the power to love, it is thou who knowest how much thou hast given him to love me and me to love him . . ."[1] Bernard's relations with his monks were often very charming and intimate and when he had to send a monk away to make a foundation he sometimes missed him very sorely and nearly always the monks who had left were homesick for Clairvaux. The "nostalgia Claravallensis" was a familiar complaint in new foundations.

[1] Ep. 87 (Migne 85).

"When you wring your hands, dearest Rainald," Bernard wrote to one of his sons who had become Abbot of Foigny, "over your many troubles I too am moved to tears. When you are sorrowful, I cannot but be sorry; nor can I hear of your worries and troubles without being myself worried and troubled. But as I foresaw and warned you of the very ills which you declare have befallen you, you should have been forearmed against what was foreknown so as to have endured them with a lighter heart and, if possible, spared me the vexation of hearing all about them. As it is I suffer more than enough by not having you with me, by not being able to see anything of you and enjoy the comfort of your company, so that I am at times tempted to regret having sent you away. And when, on top of all this, you, who should be a staff to support me, use your faintheartedness as a staff with which to belabour me, you are piling sadness upon sadness, one cross upon another." As a consequence of this letter Rainald stopped telling Bernard about his troubles, and then Bernard wrote to him: "I had hoped, dearest son, to find a remedy for my worrying over you in not being told of your difficulties. But now I find my anxiety for you increased by the very thing that I hoped would relieve it. Hitherto I have only feared or grieved over what you told me, but now there is hardly an evil that could happen which I do not fear for you. In fact as your favourite Ovid says: Quando ego non timui graviora pericula veris."[1] We have already noticed Bernard's intimate friendship with Peter the Venerable and we have seen how attached he became to his secretary Nicolas until he was betrayed by him.

There is very little doubt that Bernard's emotional crises and upsets had their source in the wretched state of his health. We all know how prone we are to this sort of thing, how difficult it is to see anything objectively when we are seedy, and Bernard was always a very sick man. Nevertheless he did not find it at all easy to endure fools gladly or even patiently, and he was certainly subject to sudden outbursts of irritation, apt to boil over like a saucepan of milk, and his gift for invective could make his anger rather uncomfortable for the object. A good example of his power in this direction is the letter he wrote to the Bishop of Ostia about Cardinal Jordon Orsino: "Your legate has passed 'from country to country,

---

[1] Ep. 76 (Migne 73) and Ep. 77 (Migne 74). "When have I not by fear made dangers greater than they really were?" Ovid. Ep. 1, verse 11.

the guest of king or people', leaving everywhere amongst us the foul and horrid traces of his progress. . . . It is said that he has committed foul deeds everywhere, that he has looted churches, that he has promoted good-looking youths to ecclesiastical benefices, and that where he has not done this it was not for lacking will to do so."[1] The rest of this letter is in much the same vein.

But we must not think that Bernard was forever denouncing people, rather the contrary is true. We have seen how he lost the friendship of Pope Innocent for supporting Peter of Pisa, but this is not by any means the only case of his taking up the cudgels in favour of someone who he thought had been wronged, and although he could be very severe on a man who had misbehaved he was always the first person to take up his defence if he saw true repentance and sorrow. There is a charming letter of his to Pope Eugenius on behalf of the Bishop of Orleans in which he says: "The time has now come for me to write to you on behalf of the humble and poor monk who is now no longer a bishop; and what makes it all the more sad is that he has come to this after being rich and important. . . . If I were to say that because he has humbled himself he ought to be exalted, I should not be presuming too rashly. But I do not say that he should be exalted, only that he should not be scorned. . . . Have you not the power to put down the mighty from their seats and to exalt the humble? To use power only against evil without using it also for good is to abuse it. This poor man, now that he is really poor, is worried by many debts, so command, I beg you, that they may be paid out of the episcopal revenues. It is very hard to be both deprived of honour and crushed by debt."[2] If Bernard considered that anyone had been really badly treated, then he was up in his defence and quite unconcerned what he said or to whom he said it. When Pope Eugenius deprived Samson, the Archbishop of Rheims, of the pallium on what Bernard considered to be mistaken grounds, he did not hesitate to write to him: "God forgive you, what have you done? You have put a modest man to shame; you have humiliated before the whole Church a man whom the whole Church praises."[3] But Bernard was not only concerned with the great and powerful, we have seen how he befriended John of Salisbury and Robert Pullen when they

[1] Ep. 355 (Migne 290).
[2] Ep. 322 (Migne 246).
[3] Ep. 323 (Migne 247).

were both poor and unknown, and there is a charming letter of his in favour of the Abbot of Châtillon who had lost his pigs: "That very good man the Abbot of Châtillon left all his property under my protection when he set out for Rome. And now the servants of Simon, men of Belfort, have taken off his pigs. I assure you I would sooner have had my own pigs stolen . . ." he wrote to Count Henry, son of Theobald, Count of Champagne and went on to beg him to use his influence to get the abbot's pigs restored to him. There are also countless short letters of his that are quite enchanting for their kindly humour. He was always writing to abbots of various houses on behalf of monks who had got themselves into trouble in one way or another and were afraid to return to their monasteries, of which the following to Berald, Abbot of St. Ben-ignus, Dijon, is typical: "I appeal to your loving heart for this little sheep of yours who has strayed from the fold. I beg you to have mercy and compassion on him after the example of the Good Shep-herd. I know full well how capricious he is, I know that he has left his monastery twice before this and been received back. Neverthe-less your paternity knows very well that mercy must be preferred to justice, and Blessed Benedict, who says that a monk is to be received back up to three times, is especially to be obeyed. It is for this that Brother Henry implores your kindness."[1]

Perhaps one of the most endearing things about Bernard was his impish humour. It sparkles all through his letters and in many of his sermons and, needless to say, it was not always understood by the pompous ecclesiastics and devout people of his day. To appreciate his humour fully we need to see it in its context, but there is one enchanting short note which he wrote to the Bishop of Noyon, a rather self-important prelate:

"To the lord Baldwin, Bishop of Noyon, something better than he deserves, from Brother Bernard styled Abbot of Clairvaux. I am sending you this small boy who is bringing this letter to eat your bread so that I may discover from the sort of welcome you give him whether you are really mean. The tone of this letter will have to serve as my seal because it is not to hand, neither is my secretary, your Godfrey."[2] Clearly the humorous tone of this letter was sufficient indication that it came from Bernard. There is also the well-known letter to the Pope warning him not to be taken in

[1] Ep. 234. Text edited by Hüffer.
[2] Ep. 434 (Migne 402).

by the "crocodile tears" of a certain bishop who was coming to see him.

Bernard must have been the most lovable of Superiors, more of a companion and father to his monks than a high and mighty abbot, at any rate after experience had taught him that not every monk could or should be like himself. If we had visited him at Clairvaux there is no doubt that we should have been quite enthralled by the charm and force of his personality, by his kindly humour, and by the interest he took in the every-day details of our rather ordinary life. We should have been astonished at his self-effacement and modesty and by the apparently unlimited time he had for our affairs. Undoubtedly he would have been brim-full of gaiety and would have made us feel not only at ease but also as if we were really rather good and important people. He seemed to have the gift of bringing the best out of everyone; even the most truculent were shamed into good behaviour in his company. Only if we were a little pompous and self-important would we have felt rather uncomfortable with him, uncertain whether his humour was directed at us or not. Nor does he seem to have been at all autocratic with his monks; there are many instances of his following the advice of his community against his own judgement, and there is an amusing letter, discovered by Dom Jean Leclercq, the greatest of all living authorities on Bernard, in which he says that he is returning the dogs which had been given him because his monks, in view of the donor's evil life, would not let him keep them; and we have seen how on the insistence of his monks he reinstated one of them whom in a fit of temper he had turned out of the community.

What was Bernard's secret? What was the secret of his enormous influence in his own day and how is it that even now, eight hundred years after his death, he still speaks to the hearts of men and draws them after him "in the odour of his ointments"? It is interesting to compare him with his contemporary Henry de Blois, the Bishop of Winchester. Henry de Blois came from a very great family indeed and he was undoubtedly a massive personality and considerable scholar. Yet Henry de Blois is just a name in history, doubtless a fascinating and great character, but quite dead whereas Bernard is still alive. The secret lies, of course, in Bernard's sanctity, his enormous charity, and complete singleness of purpose. Henry de Blois was a great statesman and ambitious, Bernard too was a statesman and ambitious, but he was first and foremost a monk and a man of God; he was ambitious, but only for the glory of God and the good estate of the Church. Like Henry de Blois, Bernard came of a great family and like him he was highly endowed by nature, but the difference is that Bernard was a Saint. By this we do not mean that he was free of all human frailty but simply that he was a man in love with God and, because in love with God, in love also with his fellow men. In all his many activities there was no atom of self-seeking or self-aggrandizement. No sooner was his work done than he immediately returned to his plough. In spite of his appalling health he never seems to have refused any of the demands made upon him; he even left his death-bed to try to bring peace to men, and God knows what this must have cost him. He was nervous and highly strung, but he did not allow this to distract him by one iota from his purpose or to deflect him from his duty as he conceived it; on the contrary by his great love he was able to harness his very faults and physical ills in the service of God and man. He may have been hard on men like Abelard and he may have been mistaken, but there was nothing petty about him, nothing mean, and he was never hard on anyone except for what he believed to be the ultimate good of the Church and the man himself. Let the most abandoned sinner, the most tiresome and querulous heretic, show but one sign of right purpose and Bernard is immediately at his side to help him. He is a classic example of a man who found his life by losing it. As a youth he gave up all his cherished ambitions of literary fame and eminence to bury himself in a poor and obscure monastery where, by all human calculations, he would never be heard of again, but through this very act of heroic surrender and generosity he was able to achieve a fame and influence that have endured for eight hundred years and show no signs of waning.

FINIS

BIBLIOGRAPHY

Vitae Sancti Bernardi Abbatis: auctore Gulielmo olim S. Theoderici, Ernaldo Abbate Bonae-Vallis in Agro Carnutensi, Gaufrido monacho quondam Clarae-Vallensi, Alano quondam episcopo Autisioderensi, Joanne Eremita.

Exordium Magnum Cisterciense.

Statuta Capitulorum Generalium Ordinis Cisterciensis. Josephus Canivez. Louvain. 1933.

Sancti Bernardi Abbatis Opera Omnia. Parisiis. M.DCC.XIX.

The Letters of Saint Bernard of Clairvaux newly translated by Bruno S. James. Burns and Oates.

Vie de Saint Bernard. Vacandard. Paris. 1927.

Saint Bernard of Clairvaux. Watkin Williams. Manchester University Press. 1935.

Saint Bernard. Joseph Calmette et Henri David. Librairie Artheme Fayard. Paris. 1953.

Der Heilige Bernard. Hüffer.

Bernard de Clairvaux. Commission d'Histoire de l'Ordre de Citeaux. Abbaye de Notre Dame d'Aiguebelle. Editions Alsatia. Paris 1953.

Guillaume de St. Thierry. André Adam.

Guillaume de St. Thierry. J. M. Dechanet.

Commentarius de Scriptoribus Ecclesiasticis. Leipzig.

Vita Ludovicii Grossi. Suger. Migne.

Five Centuries of Religion. Coulton. Cambridge University Press. 1923.

St. Bernard. Morrison.

Saint Bernard of Clairvaux. Richard Storrs. Hodder & Stoughton. 1892.

Citeaux and her Elder Daughters. Archdale King. Burns & Oates.

Historie de l'Eglise. Fliche.

Mélange St. Bernard. XXIV Congèrs de l'Association Bourguiguonne de Sociétés Savantes. Dijon. 1953.

Etudes sur St. Bernard. D. Jean Leclercq. Analecta Sacri Ordinis Cisterciensis. 1953. Fasc: 1–2.

Mystical Theology of St. Bernard. Gilson. Sheed & Ward.

Joannis Salisburensis: Historia Pontificalis.

David Knowles: The Case of St. William of York. *Cambridge Historical Journal*. Vol. II (1936). 162–77, 212–14.

David Knowles: The Monastic Order in England. Cambridge University Press.

Louis Bouyer: La Spiritualité de Citeaux. Au Portulan. Paris.

The Writings of Saint Bernard

The Letters: During the year 1145 Bernard's secretary, Geoffrey of Auxerre, collected and published three hundred of his letters. This represented only a fragment of the whole for Bernard's correspondence must have been large. The researches of Mabillon, Martene, and Durand have considerably added to this collection, and since their time such scholars as Hüffer in last century and Dom Jean Leclercq and Dr. Talbot in our own day have augmented it still further.

Treatise on the Degrees of Humility and Pride: This is the first of Bernard's treatises and was written some time between the years 1121 and 1125 in response to the request of his prior, Geoffrey, to embody the gist of his sermons on the subject in the form of a book. It is the most readable and, in some ways, the most characteristic of all Bernard's formal treatises. He has illustrated the degrees of pride with superb pen-portraits, obviously drawn from life, of which the following is a typical example. Describing a monk in the seventh degree of pride, of which the characteristic is presumption, he writes: "How can a monk who thinks he excels others not suppose himself better than others? Such an one takes the first place in community meetings; in council he is always the first to answer; he pushes himself forward uninvited; he interferes without authority; he re-arranges what has already been arranged; he does all over again what has already been done once. He sits in judgement on his superiors and passes judgement on others before judgement has been given. If, when the time comes, he is not made prior, he thinks his abbot is deceived in him or that he is jealous of him; if he is told to do some small thing he is outraged and gets on his high horse believing himself above such trifling matters and fit only for great affairs."

The Love of God: One of the most popular of all Bernard's writings, this small work was written about the year 1127 for Cardinal Haimeric. The beginning is famous: "You asked me why we should love God and how much we should love him. I reply that we should love God because he is God and that the measure of our love should be to love him without measure."

On Precept and Dispensation: A rather specialized treatise written in answer to the question of some monks whether the Holy Rule of Saint Benedict was binding under pain of sin. It treats of obedience and monastic perfection.

The Apology: Perhaps the most quoted if not the most widely read of all

Bernard's treatises. Written at the request of William of St. Thierry in defence of the Cistercian movement and the author's own position with regard to the Black Monks.

On the Life and Duties of a Bishop: Written for the Archbishop of Sens, Henry the Wild Boar, soon after his conversion. In it Bernard warns Henry against luxury, ambition, and a too aggressive spirit of independence, and he takes the opportunity to speak his mind on abbots who ape bishops by wearing mitres and rings.

On Conversion: A sermon preached to the students of Paris and published by Bernard in the form of a short treatise.

In Praise of the New Warfare to the Knights of the Temple: The name of this treatise is self-explanatory.

Against the Errors of Abelard: A polemical work lacking the serenity of Bernard's other treatises but closely reasoned and still useful.

On Monastic Chant: A long letter prefacing the Reformed Cistercian Antiphonary in which Bernard enlarges on the nature of monastic chant.

The Life of Saint Malachy: Hagiography after the fashion of the times.

On Consideration: An early book of meditation written for Pope Eugenius III. Of practical use even in the present day and for others besides Popes.

Sermons: Numerous sermons, some in praise of Our Blessed Lady, others for the seasons of the year and feasts of the Saints. It is unlikely that all these sermons were preached in the form in which we have them, almost certainly Bernard edited them for publication. In the short "Sermons on Various Subjects" we are nearer the actual preaching of Bernard.

On the Song of Songs: A collection of eighty-four sermons on the Song of Songs supposed to have been preached by Bernard to his monks. Modern scholars are doubtful whether they were ever actually preached, partly because of their great length and partly because of the difficult nature of the subject. It seems unlikely that even at Clairvaux there were many monks able to follow long Latin sermons on such an abstruse matter. Bernard is concerned with the mystical meaning of the text and all of the sermons are of great depth and beauty. In them we have Bernard's most mature spiritual teaching and they are rightly considered his most important work.

INDEX

Abelard, Peter, 13, 134 seq.
Adam, monk of Morimond, 61 seq.
Ailred of Rievaulx, St., 144, 178
Alba, Bishop of, 119
Alberic of Rheims, 93
Alberic, St., 28 seq.
Aleth, mother of Bernard, 17, 20, 24
Alexander, Bishop of Lincoln, 77
Amadeus I, Count of Geneva, 88
Anacletus, *v.* Peter Leon
Andrew, brother of Bernard, 25, 32, 40
Anselm of Laon, 135
Arnold, Abbot of Morimond, 59 seq.
Arnold of Bonneval, 108
Arnold of Brescia, 141

Baldwin, Abbot of Rieti, 84
Bamberg, diet of, 119
Bartholomew, brother of Bernard, 25
Basil, St., 43 note
Benedict, St., Holy Rule, *passim*
Benedict, monk of St. Germer de Flay, 65 seq.
Berengarius, 19
Bernard de Brancion, Prior of Cluny, 45 seq.
Bernard of Clairvaux, St., as Abbot, 80 seq., 182
accepts monks from other houses, 64 seq.
activities, 97, 105, 183
apologia, 52 seq., 57
and Apostolic See, 88
appearance and character, 41, 176 seq.

birth, 11
and the Church, 86 seq.
and contemplative life, 86 seq.
composure and serenity, 35
controversy with Abelard, 134 seq.
controversy with Gilbert de la Porrée, 170
and the Crusade, 161 seq.
and Roman Curia, 98
death of, 11, 175
duplicity of, 155
education of, 18 seq.
at council of Etampes, 106
fame of, 161
family of, 17 seq.
his genius for friendship, 178
his mission to the Genoese, 111 seq.
his weak health, 36 seq.
his home, 17
his humility, 89
his humour, 181
in Italy, 110
his gift for invective, 179
his protection of Jews, 165
and the Langres election, 127 seq.
his love of learning, 134
his letter to Robert, 46
on the love of God, 71 seq.
his miracles, 39
his mission to Milan, 120
his nostalgia for Clairvaux, 118 seq.
novice at Citeaux, 30 seq.
ordination and blessing, 34
and the papacy, 121